The ULTIMATE *You*

3 month planner

Create happiness within yourself and the outside world will follow

tellwell

Tellwell Talent
www.tellwell.ca

ISBN
978-0-2288-0075-0 (Hardcover)
978-0-2288-0074-3 (Paperback)

Author's Note

Thank you so much for taking the first step towards becoming the ULTIMATE YOU!

I am so excited about the changes you are about to experience and I cannot wait to learn about the incredible gifts you will bring into the world once you become the ULTIMATE YOU!

I am confident you were born for greatness—that all of us are born to become our very best selves. Each of us has something special in us just waiting to emerge. This book will help YOU become the best possible version of yourself and will give you the tools to change your entire life so it evolves into its greatest potential too.

Now is the time!

Monthly Charity Giveaway!

By purchasing this book, not only will you create lasting positive effects in your own life, but you will create positivity in the world as well. Twenty-five percent of proceeds from *The Ultimate You* will be donated to a charity of (potentially) your choice. Each month a new charity, society or service group will be chosen to receive the donation.

If you have a particular charity or organization that you would like to see benefit from sales of *The Ultimate You,* Email your suggestion, along with **your name** and the **full name and address** of the organization to:

the.ultimate.you@outlook.com

You will receive an email if the organization you suggested is the chosen recipient.

Thanks for making a difference!

Introduction

Welcome to the first day of the rest of your ultimate—and successful—life!

To get the most out of this book, not to mention the very best out of yourself and your life, you must think of it as your new best friend.

You know what I mean: this book must become the friend you want to do everything with; the friend you tell your secrets to and brainstorm ideas with; the friend you work out and discuss your diet with; the buddy you share what you're thankful for with; and, of course, that special person you talk with about all the amazing things that happen to you every single day! By no means should this book *replace* your human best friends; it's just a nice addition to your group.

This book is your accountability partner. In partnership with this book, you will reflect at the end of every day on your accomplishments and achievements—and your new best friend is not going to lie to you; it will tell you exactly how much effort you're putting into each area of your life.

The effort you put into consistently using the tools in this book will impact your life. Hopefully the amount of check marks and ink all over the pages will make you proud and leave you feeling like you've accomplished the most and best you possibly could at the end of every day.

I wish you all the success, happiness, joy, love and bliss you've ever dreamed of. I truly believe with all my heart that, after diving into this lifestyle, if you persevere, keep an open mind and a positive outlook, you will achieve your dreams at an unbelievable rate.

I believe this with my whole heart because I did it myself, I completely turned around my *own* life! When I started my journey to success I was completely lost. I had just broken up with my partner of six years and was living in my parent's basement. I was working at a job that no longer brought me joy. I weighed more than I had ever weighed in my entire life. I had no energy, no drive and just felt stuck. I decided I wanted more, I deserved more and I sure-as-shit was going to *be* more!

So, I started researching, reading, meditating and following the habits of all the great achievers of the world. Within a short amount of time I realized that the events in my life were not happening *to* me, they were happening *through* me and if I wanted a different world on the outside, I needed to create a different world on the inside.

So, instead of looking at all that was wrong in my world, I started looking at all the things in my life I was grateful for. When I started paying tribute to all I was grateful for, more and more positive things started appearing in my life every day.

It was incredible! I quickly fell in love with myself and life again. Magically, my perfect partner came into my life. Together we built a beautiful home and we travel the world.

But even better, my life transformed to the point that I was able to quit my job to pursue my passions and dreams; I am full of energy and in the best shape of my life; I have time for family members; I am finally training for a marathon, one of my bucket list items that I almost wrote off— *and* I get to make my own schedule! Boy, do I ever feel blessed every morning when I wake up!

I am living the life of my dreams and I have the good habits I learned while creating and refining the processes outlined in this book—to thank for it. I truly hope what I have learned has the same effect on your life; I want this for you, you deserve it!

So, a toast to you for taking the first step!

To all that you have been, all that you are right now and all that you can and will be in the near future. I love you! Now go, get started!

1. User Guide:

A page-by-page explanation of how to get the most out of this planner

Affirmations and Routines

Read Section 1 as much as possible. It is full of **positive affirmations** I've selected to help you start your day in a wonderful way. Section 1 contains gentle reminders that every day we learn a little more, we love a little more, we get one step closer to our true self and one step closer to realizing our dreams!

- **The message from Karena and Katrina** from **toneitup.com** is a guaranteed way to succeed in every aspect of your life. If you look for love everywhere you go, in everything you do and in everyone you see, then a fulfilling and successful life is inevitable. Tone It Up is a fitness website I stumbled upon years ago. Those girls completely inspired me to change the way that I think about working out, fitness and nutrition.

- **The beautiful message from Norma Oliver** 🖤 (aka Nan) is a combination of words and actions that will change your life (if you commit to live by them). Nan was the most incredible, strong, kind, loving and motivating woman I have ever met. I was so blessed to have her as my grandmother for 29 years. Nan taught me the importance of family, of helping wherever you can, of being kind to everyone and being truly grateful for all the blessings life bestows. If you can be happy and appreciate where you are and what you have, then you will never feel need or longing, as all you could ever require will naturally be drawn into your life.

- **Add one little thing to your morning routine**: Sometimes we feel the need to wake up and hit the ground running because there are *'just not enough hours in the day'*. However, if you take the time to wake up happy, get excited and visualize exactly what you WANT to happen in the following 16 hours, I promise you that your day will flow so smoothly that you will have extra time at the end of the day—yes, you heard me—**EXTRA TIME for YOU!** So wake up and smile. Thank the universe for another beautiful day. Look in the mirror and say out loud to yourself, "I love you, you are absolutely perfect and you can do anything." Do whatever it takes to create positive energy in the morning!

- **Add one little thing to your evening routine:** What you think about, and how you feel right before you lay your head on the pillow, has a strong influence on your sleep patterns and the thoughts you wake up with in the morning. Your subconscious mind takes your last thoughts and rolls with them all night long. So why not make those ideas and feelings happy, exciting and joyous to inspire you while you sleep? Always, *always* go to bed feeling amazing—do whatever it takes! Adding this to your regular routine helps fill your mind with positive thoughts and excitement about your dreams so you can wake in the morning ready to crush it all day long!

Values & Beliefs

Section 2 is a space for you to write down your core values and beliefs. What do you want to bring forth into the world every single day? How do you want to interact with other people and with yourself? What do you value? What is important to you? Make sure that everything you write in this book is written in a **positive manner**. If there is something you know you do *not* like, then write the opposite, which is what you *do* like.

Focus on what you WANT! Always, always, *always* focus on what you want! I firmly believe that focusing on what you want is the number one secret to achieving the amazing life you deserve.

Examples of Core Values and Beliefs:

- I treat others as I wish to be treated. I am honest and trustworthy. Life is meant to be enjoyed. I finish what I start. Money comes easily to me. I always leave a place better than I found it. I always give more than I hope to receive. I am confident. I am sexy. I am love. When I follow my heart, I will find my bliss.

Please listen to your heart and write out what is important to YOU!

Life Goals

GET WILD! Dream HUGE dreams! Here are two quotes to think about before you start this section:

> "If your dreams do not scare you, they are not big enough" – Ellen Johnson Sirleaf

> "The ONLY limitation is the one you set up in your own mind" – Napoleon Hill

The world needs what you have to offer and you deserve to be who you want to be, do what you want to do and have what you want to have. This is your chance to get creative, to get real, to listen to your heart and to become the ULTIMATE YOU.

Any dream is possible—JUST WRITE IT DOWN! Dr. Gail Matthews, a psychology professor at the Dominican University in California, did a study of the art and science of goal setting. Her findings show that if you write down a goal or dream (and continue to do so) you are 42 percent more likely to achieve it! WHAT? Just by writing out your dreams and really thinking about what you want, your chances of making your dreams a reality increase by 42 percent! Awesome!

Get clear on what you want from your life in the following areas:

Health & Fitness – What do you want to look and feel like? Define your weight goals, nutrition goals and fitness goals—for example, if you are a runner, define what you want to achieve with distance and endurance.

Love & Relationships – What does your perfect love relationship look like? How would you like your family relationships to manifest? What does your social life look like?

Career & Business – How much money do you make? Do you own your own company? Did you make partner in your firm? Are you a great investor? What service are you providing to the world in exchange for money?

There are approximately 7.6 *billion* people on earth right now. I guarantee that thousands, if not millions, of them want to read, use, wear, learn, or eat whatever it is that you want to create. Even if it has been done before, it has not been done BY YOU before and that is what makes your product or service different. You are not in competition with anyone, there is and can be abundance for all! With the power of the internet and a global marketplace, there are so many different ways to reach out and promote your dream. You just need to decide you're going to do it!

This is *YOUR* dream life – What do you want?

Remember what Napoleon said: "The only limitation is the one you set up in your own mind."

Philanthropy & Giving Back – Every truly wealthy individual knows that one of the greatest parts about having an abundance of money is the ability to give back and help the world become a better place. Is there a certain organization, group or charitable society you would like to get involved with? Do you want to start your own? How can you make a difference?

Material Things & Experiences – What kind of car do you drive? What does your house look like? What toys do you want to own? Where do you want to travel to? What do you want to see and experience? You deserve to have everything that you have ever wanted and digging into Section 3 is your chance to get detailed about it all (and be sure to use extra paper if your creative juices get flowing and you run out of room)!

In Section 4, you will take these life goals and illustrate them with a masterful vision board!

Vision Board

Remember, writing down your goals increases your odds of success by 42 percent. So turning your written goals into pictures on a board that inspire the feeling of having, doing or being what you desire can only increase that number. In the next five pages, build your vision board. Use pictures from books or the Internet, draw doodles or figures that represent what you wish to achieve, find magazine clippings or quotes that inspire you—the options are endless! Just be creative and visually express the words you wrote for each of the categories you created on page 3.

I have made numerous vision boards in my life and it constantly amazes me to see how well they work and just how many dreams I have manifested into my reality. Vision boards truly work! The book (and movie) The Secret says that **Visualization is one of the most powerful mind exercises you can do.** So having your vision board in a special place that you will see multiple times in a day is a sure way towards success in all your dreams and desires.

The key to successfully using a vision board is to put your heart and soul into making it, then immerse yourself into those feelings whenever you see it. Think of the vision board as the new reality of your life. Absorb its power. Do this daily and project as much detail as possible into envisioning your achievements. How is it going to feel when you cross the finish line at your first marathon? What colour and model is your new truck and what air freshener hangs from the mirror? Get as many senses involved as you can—movement, colour, sounds and smells.

As you accomplish your goals, set new ones! Make sure to update your vision board regularly.

Three-Month Goals

Once you have created your dream life, take a look at the different areas of it and break them down into achievable parts. Perhaps you decided your dream is to write a book. What can you do in the next three months to get in line with that goal? Maybe you could set a goal to write one chapter, or pick an idea for the book. Maybe you can create a title page— or just come up with the title! It just takes one step in the direction of your dream to get the ball rolling, so what are you waiting for?

For example, if you are a runner like me, maybe your dream is to run a marathon, so your goal for the next three months could be to get out and walk every day, or even every other day. Try downloading an app, such as 'couch – 10k' or 'couch – marathon' and start training. Find an accountability partner (someone else who has the same goal) to motivate you—it always helps to have a partner! Buy yourself your marathon outfit and hang it in your closet so you can be inspired by it every day! Or get really wild and register for your marathon!

The key is to take action on whatever it is you are working toward! And be consistent—make sure to take action every day. Even the smallest action toward your goal will help it become reality.

Do you want to start a company? Start looking for the perfect location for your business! Do you have a business plan in place? Create your logo! Decide what kind of music you want to play—what vibe is your business going to put out? Do you have a name you could register to make it a legitimate company?

How about your relationships? Do you want to have a more positive relationship with yourself? Make a goal that for the next three months you will compliment yourself every single day. Take yourself on a date! Do whatever it is that brings your heart joy.

You do not have to make a huge financial investment or life-altering change right away. Just make a goal for each of the five areas of life previously discussed and get going on your path to success and complete bliss.

One-Year Goals

Once you've accomplished your three-month goals, it's time to start pushing a little more. I learned a really cool visualization tool from Dean Graziosi. He says to picture yourself one year from today looking back at the very best year of your life: What happened? What did you achieve? Where did you go? How did you feel?

At the end of one year, maybe you have completed a draft copy of your book or five chapters—only you know your schedule!

At the end of one year, perhaps you are going to participate in that marathon you registered for, or you can easily run 15 kilometres.

At the end of one year, maybe you've completed your business plan and have the life-sized business sign with your logo on it sitting in your living room—a constant reminder that you are getting so close!

At the end of the year, you see yourself smiling every time you look in the mirror and you say to yourself, **"Damn, you are looking fine!"**

Making Dreams Happen and Adding Income Streams

Change can be uncomfortable, but discomfort is just a reminder that you are one step closer to doing everything you've ever wanted to do and being everything you've ever wanted to be!

Section 7 is a reminder that it is normal to have strange feelings and it's okay to be scared. Remember that your fears are generated by the *old* you, who wants to keep you right where you are: in comfortable, familiar territory. The *real* you is pushing through, growing and evolving! Keep doing that! feel the fear, love the fear, walk through it and keep going! Fear means you are close to your dreams. Stay focused on what you want—let go of what others want for you or think is right for you. FOLLOW **YOUR HEART** on **YOUR PATH!** Soon people will applaud you and want to know your secrets!

This section is for you to think of some cool ways to produce extra income. Having numerous income streams allows you to relax a little when it comes to money; if one stream slows down a little, it's okay because you're brilliant and have other (at least four!) income streams delivering money.

Almost everything has a cost and that's okay. Material goods (things) cost money. Business start-ups cost money. Traveling costs money. Your dream house costs money. Money is a great thing and it is fabulous to have money!

Affirm that money flows to you easily and effortlessly to you and then start thinking of ways to achieve it that are suitable for *you*. Do you want to sell a book you wrote? Do you enjoy yard clean-up and want to advertise your services on Kijiji? Do you like walking dogs? Do you have a new business idea? Do you have investments or real estate income? Want to try out being an Uber driver?

There are unlimited ways to make money. Make sure you choose things that bring you joy! If you do things because they make you happy, you can be sure the dollars will appear.

Have faith in the infinite universe; there is more than enough wealth and happiness for everybody!

My 'Why'

I hope you are feeling motivated, excited and have a deep knowing in your soul that **YOU** were born to be the **ULTIMATE YOU. YOU** were born to be happy and filled with bliss and joy. **YOU** deserve everything you have ever wanted.

The previous section, Section 7, is about how to achieve things, but the 'why' of achieving is just as important—perhaps more so—than the 'how'. The 'why' gives meaning and purpose to your mission: Why do you want to be successful? Why do you want to be in the best shape of your life? Why do you want to find the perfect partner?

Once you write down *why* you feel a burning desire to live the life of your dreams, you can use that statement to remind yourself to keep going when you feel like you're drifting off course. If you have an 'off day' or need a little inspiration and encouragement to get up at 5:30 a.m. to squeeze in a run before work then your 'why' message will give you the push and motivation to get up and own it!

Your 'why' will motivate you to keep going when your mind is temporarily confused and telling you it's too hard. So make sure your 'why' is powerful enough to drive you into bringing out the ULTIMATE YOU!

Day to day planner

Gratitude

One of the most important habits you can ever form is practising gratitude each and every day. There have been many studies done on the beneficial effects of giving thanks and feeling gratitude. *How Gratitude Changes You and Your Brain* by Joel Wong and Joshua Brown discuss different ideas on how gratitude not only impacts how you feel in your day-to-day life, but it also has lasting physical and mental benefits, even if you are just writing things down and keeping it to yourself! Gratitude is a game changer.

In this section, you will write down all the things you are grateful for. You can do this in point form by making a list of the many things you are grateful for in this life, or you can pick one specific thing you are grateful for and explain why you feel gratitude for it today.

Do whatever your heart desires! Do this every single day! Make it a habit: write out your grateful feelings for the many different things, people, places and activities in your world that enhance your life each day.

Personal GRATITUDE: Are you grateful for your health, mind or material things? We are so incredibly blessed just to be alive that this list could go on forever.

Love & Relationships GRATITUDE: Are you grateful for your spouse, family, friends, mail-man, co-worker or pets? How about the man who held the door open for you at the grocery store?

Professional GRATITUDE: Are you grateful for your job? Has your boss given you special recognition? Is your professional life providing you with rewards in the way of money and career opportunities?

Life GRATITUDE: Write down anything and everything you see as positive in your life! Your cat, your new running shoes, the friend who called to wish you a happy birthday—anything that comes to mind!

 # 1 Priority for the day

Write down the most important thing you need to do today to bring you one step closer to accomplishing your dream. After you write it down, focus on it and get it done!

I am going to focus and improve on …

Next write down anything you wish to improve, from your form at the gym, to how you talk to your kids or spouse, to smiling at strangers or being present or more patient—anything you want to personally improve on.

What can I do to make a difference?

Think about and decide how you can make the world a better place *today* and write it down! Remember, writing things down is a technique that makes us 42 percent more likely to achieve our goals!

Do you have a friend you want to help? Could you pick up some garbage off the street and put it in a bin? Can you make an effort to smile at every person you meet, hold doors open, or compliment others you encounter? Every positive thing you do in a day has a ripple effect that you can't even begin to imagine. Spread **love** and feel it radiating back to you!

Daily Reflection

At the end of the day as you get ready for bed, do whatever it is that helps you relax, and especially—*turn the screens off!*

Once you are relaxed, review your day and write out all the amazing things that happened. Maybe you looked SMOKIN' in your outfit today; maybe traffic was easy on your way to work; perhaps your favourite song played on the radio or you did something really awesome at work and had a big breakthrough. Or you had the world's greatest workout, your partner did something sweet, or you did something sweet for your partner!

There are so many things that can go *right* in a day; write them all out here. This will help bring out amazing feelings before you hit the hay and will allow your subconscious to propel you to the next level for tomorrow.

If something didn't go your way during your day, get creative and visualize how you wish it had gone then LET IT GO. Feel the negative energy from that experience leave your body. Feel the release and move on.

For example, if you spilled coffee on yourself because you were rushing to an appointment you could write: Tomorrow I am going to be very organized, I am going to have time to enjoy my coffee AND I am going to get everywhere I need to go with ease.

Remember, the key to life is focusing on what you *want* to happen, not reliving the stuff you didn't like.;)

Food Journal

The food journal is for tracking what we put in our mouths! Successful people love to treat their bodies with respect, they love to feel good and look good and a huge part of that is how we fuel our body!

What we eat and when we eat influences how much energy we have, how clearly we are thinking and how much we can get done in a day. The food/drinks we ingest have a huge effect on our physical body, affecting, for example, skin tone and elasticity and even the brightness of our eyes; but a poor diet can also affect our moods and energy levels as well. Definitely continue to treat yourself to those things you really love, but make sure that the majority of the time you are spoiling yourself with delicious and *nutritious* foods.

Exercise Journal

Exercise feels amazing and will help you *look* amazing. Exercise brings high levels of oxygen into your body which enhances mood, boosts energy, promotes better sleep, allows you to think more clearly, turns you into a better problem solver and even improves your sex life: how could you not do this for yourself *EVERY DAY!?*

In this section, record what exercises you are doing. Doing multiple types of exercise in one day is awesome. It doesn't have to be at a gym: go for a walk, stretch, do a workout online, go to a yoga class, chase your kids around the house for half an hour—anything, as long as you're moving! Write it all down so you can look at all the great things you are doing for your body and then take a moment to celebrate your accomplishments!

** Helpful hint – Exercising first thing in the morning is believed to increase your metabolism, helping to burn fat and keep you revved up all day. *8 Health Benefits of Morning Workouts* by Moira Lawler explains the findings of numerous studies on the effects of the morning pump. Sweating first thing in the morning energizes your mind, body and soul for the day ahead and even helps you build a mental protective wall against the sugary or unhealthy treats you're trying to cut back on. What a perfect and empowered way to start every day!

Rate your day

At the end of each day, rate each category of it! This is just a fun way to track your overall feelings and daily accomplishments. Rate your day out of 10, 1 being the world's worst day and 10 being your dream day. After about one or two weeks of following all the steps in this book, you should find your day rate rising continuously. You will soon be able to look back and see all your day rates of 8's, 9's and 10's! Get ready for the bliss.

In Western culture in particular, we are encouraged to believe success comes in the form of huge sums of money, getting promotions in our jobs by working long strenuous hours, or having numerous houses and beautiful cars. However, **true success is a feeling**. True success is love, balance, happiness and being a part of something bigger than yourself. Success is a whole bunch of great days combined to make a fabulous life. You can't *become* success; you have to *be* success, every moment of every day.

The Daily Mantra

This section contains some profound words by incredible thinkers from around the globe here for you to contemplate and use to inspire your day.

The Daily 'To Do' List

This is a list of important tasks that have been proven to boost your mood, creativity, health, wealth and basically just change your entire life ... *If* you do them consistently! If there is something you want to add to make your day even better, please add it.

1. Wake up and smile: The first task is to wake up and smile: if you smile often enough, you will rewire your brain to make positive patterns more often than it does negative ones. And changing negative thought patterns into positive ones is how we change our inner world, which affects who we are in the world around us! It is possible to retrain your brain so it remains in a heightened state of positivity and optimism, but it takes continuous awareness of your thoughts, words and actions. Make sure you chose them wisely! Smiling is free, contagious, feels good, is almost effortless and can be done anywhere. Smiling when you first wake up will start your day in the very best way!

2. Walk/Run: Get up and get moving! One of the very best ways to get pumped up for the day is to wake up, smile and then get your butt outside. Whether you run, jog or walk, get that blood moving, take in that fresh air, wake up your brain and take in all the beauty this world has to offer. This is where the magic happens; this is where everything begins! Being outdoors will renew and refresh your mind, body and soul.

3. Gratitude: Fill out the gratitude section in this book! Nothing will stand in the way of a grateful heart.

4. Read and Learn: reading and learning are essential tools for happiness. If you are constantly growing, striving for more and challenging yourself, you will be excited to wake up every morning and raring to see what is in store for you that day. Be cautious about the information you are taking in and make sure it serves you in a positive way. Skip the news and negative social media feeds. What you let into your mind has a huge impact on your mood, energy and overall well-being, so keep it positive!

5. Meditate. Meditation is such a beautiful thing. Whether your meditation is simply sitting quietly for three to five minutes before the rest of the house wakes up, or you are fully present in the shower, feeling every drop of water touch your body while repeating your chosen affirmation, just take some time to completely relax, be present and give your mind and brain a little break. A few moments of meditation is like a cleansing session that freshens your mind so that new, amazing ideas have room to enter and grow.

6. Make your bed! I was absolutely shocked when I started researching this. There have been numerous articles written on the positive effects of making your bed each day, such as ***People Who Make Their Beds In The Morning Are Happier And More Productive*** by Zainab Mudallal and ***After I Read This, I Started to Make My Bed Very Willingly Every Morning*** Jennifer

<u>Wasylenko</u>. Almost all of them demonstrate that people who made their bed first thing in the morning were happier, felt accomplished first thing in the morning and were more productive throughout the entire day! Wowza, simple step – awesome results. Remember, success is not a huge gain that happens overnight, it is a combination of small habits built up over time that encourage and allow you to *be* success.

7. Donate. This is so very important. Not only do we receive what we put out into the universe but also, if you have the time, money or goods to help someone else who is less fortunate, why the heck wouldn't you? Helping others, coming together to build stronger communities and countries, that is what we were born to do. Help doesn't need to be monetary. You can help a neighbour, pick up some garbage or have a meaningful conversation with someone in need. Any kind of help makes the world a better place! Just give back.

8. Exercise and stretch. We have one body for our entire lives and we need to do everything we possibly can to take care of it. Our bodies enable us to work, allow us to play with our kids, grandkids and friends. Our bodies take us on vacation, build houses, plant gardens and take us hiking. Our bodies create the energy we need to execute the perfect days, dates and moments that we will remember for the rest of our lives. Our bodies are our most important assets, that is for sure. Exercise also increases energy, clears the mind, encourages growth and the ability to manage our emotions—**and** it helps us look fantastic in our favourite jeans.

9. Thank someone every day, whether it's the waitress who served you at lunch, the author of the fabulous book you read, a friend, family member, or the owner of a store that you love, anyone at all—just send the love out there! You can make a phone call, email, write a letter or card or even a quick text if you're short on time, but just make sure to thank the people around you for making your life better.

10. Prepare for tomorrow, tonight! Plan out the major focus for the day, the one step that is going to get you closer to your goal. Write in any appointments, meetings and deadlines you have. Schedule in your work outs, special time with your family and of course time for YOU. When you go to sleep (at a reasonable hour) knowing you have a plan for the next day you will wake up with an unexplainable energy. Also, besides just writing out your plan for tomorrow, take it one step further and physically get prepared. Get your work-out clothes picked out, your alarm set, make sure you've organized everything you need to take to the office and your keys are hanging where they belong. Preparing at night creates a calm and relaxed morning!

11. Journaling! Journaling gives you an opportunity to reflect on the day you just had. You get to relive the moments that made you smile and feel grateful. Maybe there were things in your day that didn't go exactly as you would have liked them to. Journaling lets you re-write those things so they unfold as you want them to. If you do this, the next time the unwanted situation occurs, your brain will go back to this planning session and deliver the outcome you *want*. Going to sleep with happy, excited and grateful thoughts is a huge factor in waking up in a positive frame of mind the next day, because your subconscious mind will dream about things you want or love. What you think about, you bring about!

12. Visualization! When you visualize, you look at the gorgeous pages you created based on your dream life and goals. Look at those pages and picture yourself as having those things

now. Picture your perfect house, career, spouse, vacations, cars, adventures, income ... as well as how you get involved and give back to the world—your dream world is all right here! The more you connect to your emotions when you look at these pages, the faster your dreams are going to come into your life.

13. Drink lots of water! Water flushes out unnecessary toxins in the body, keeps your skin and hair looking fabulous and even aids in weight loss. A lot of times when we feel hungry we are just thirsty;) The perks of drinking water are endless. Drink up!

Daily Calendar

The daily calendar included in this book is the space to do your daily preparations! Use it to track appointments, hot dates, birthdates and all other things that you have going on

Daily Focus

It is a great reminder to have your daily focus written in your calendar and in front of your face all day long. The more you think about it the more likely it is to get done and the closer you will be to having your dreams come true!

People to Contact

In this section, write out who you need to text, e-mail, call, skype or otherwise contact. Connection with other people is crucial for success! Let's network!

Daily 'To Do'

This is an area to jot down things that you need to remember. Or write down ideas/thoughts that come to you that you want to explore more thoroughly later. At the end of the day, if there is something not crossed off, or without a checkmark beside it, transfer it to the following day's 'to do' list.

Sundays

This is a special day! It's a day to reflect on all the amazing things you did the previous week, as well as plan for the week ahead.

It's also a great day for meal preparation. Meal prep is super important! We all get busy during the week and can sometimes wind up turning to quick, packaged food instead of fueling our bodies and minds properly. Meal prep makes life so much easier; healthy food is pre-chopped, cooked or prepped and stored in the fridge, just waiting for you to dig in and enjoy the delicious benefits!

Sunday is also a chance to look at your goals and where you are in relation to them. Then, after celebrating how far you've come, plan to take another small (or giant) step towards them! YOU are able to make all your dreams come true and you are definitely on the right track. Keep up the great work! I look forward to hearing from you when you accomplish them! I love to publish success stories on my website!

This book also provides a weekly challenge for Sundays. Just as the Daily Mantra is related to the weeks focus, so are the weekly challenges. They are designed to encourage growth and open your mind to a new way of living.

There are blank pages at the back of the book for you to write out your ideas and your master 'to do' list, or to do a little brainstorming and doodling.

Okay, that's it! **You did it** ☺

Now go get started.

Enjoy the moments of this beautiful journey to your dream life and
please make sure to share your successes to inspire others!

Affirmations and Routines

Look for LOVE in everything that you do and see.

Look for LOVE in all the people around you: your family, friends & strangers.

Look for LOVE within yourself.

Do everything with passion and purpose.

Live each day with intention.

Speak with love, exude love, look for love and you will
find happiness, confidence and success.

Karena & Katrina – Tone It Up.com

Be kind to one another, always keep in touch with your family, be grateful for
what you have and always try to be the best person that you can be, Amen.

The amazing, Norma Oliver

Morning Routine	Night Routine
Take a deep breath	Read over gratitude list
Be thankful	Journal
Visualize your day ahead	Mentally prepare for tomorrow
Read the next six pages	Always go to sleep with positive thoughts about your dreams

Values & Beliefs

Life Goals

Health & Fitness

Love & Relationships

Career & Business

Philanthropy & Giving Back

Material Things & Experiences

Three-Month Goals

One-Year Goals

Making Dreams Happen and Adding Income Streams

- Love the feeling of fear because it means you are about to grow
  - Get out of your comfort zone
  - Step away from the crowd
  - Follow your heart
  - Make your own path!

My 'Why'

Mindset

Have you ever heard the story about twin girls who were raised (together) by their alcoholic and abusive father?

They lived in the same house and experienced the same lifestyle and associated trauma, yet they grew up and ultimately led completely different lives.

One daughter became a very successful CEO of a fortune 500 company; she had a healthy relationship with her spouse and a beautiful family. She lived in a gorgeous home, took yearly vacations and was surrounded by loving friends and family.

The other daughter became addicted to heroin, lived in the streets and scrounged for food and money daily. Crazy, hey?

The wildest part was, during an interview, both the ladies were asked how they ended up where they were in life and they had the same response: "If you knew my father, you'd understand."

One daughter took the experience for what it was, learned from it and then created the life that she wanted. The other daughter played the victim, believed that was just how life was and didn't make the decision in her mind that SHE could have a better life. The only thing that was different for the twins was their mindset.

It is absolutely incredible how much power we hold in our minds that we do not use. Yet it is the one and only thing in the entire world that we have FULL control over—and most of the population only uses about one-tenth of its actual potential.

You can change that! You are going to focus on how to positively use your mind to bring all the happiness, bliss, love, wealth, health and abundance you could possibly desire into your life.

I truly believe the biggest and most beneficial secret to learn, use and share about life is that **Like Attracts Like**.

It is that simple. What you talk about, you bring about. What you think about, you create. Consciousness creates reality. How you act is how the world will act to you.

So when you are talking, talk about things that make you happy. When you are thinking, think about things you *want* in your life (it's easy to focus on what you do *not* want, but then more of that is going to appear, so take the time to think about what you *do* want). And finally, treat the world, treat other people, treat every living and non-living thing as YOU wish to be treated.

Do you want to be treated with respect? Show respect to everyone and everything. Do you want love in your life? Then give love to everyone and everything. Do you want to be treated with kindness? Then be kind to everyone and everything. That's it!

This one step, if you can remember to constantly live by it, will change everything you've ever known to be true and create a whole new world you never knew existed.

Book recommendations
The Travelers Gift – Andy Andrews
The Secret – Rhonda Byrne
Way of the Peaceful Warrior – Dan Millman

YouTube
Quantum Physics Confirms: Consciousness Creates Reality – WeAreCreators

<u>Affirmation</u>
"My thoughts become things, so I will choose them wisely."

Gratitude

Personal
_____

Love & Relationships
_____

Professional
_____

Life
_____

#1 Priority to get me one step closer to achieving my main goal is:
_____

I am going to focus and improve on:
_____

Today is the first day of the rest of my beautiful life, what am I going to do to make a difference?
_____

Daily Reflection

Food Journal

Breakfast
Snack
Lunch
Snack
Dinner
Other

Exercise

RATE YOUR DAY

PERSONAL   LOVE   WORK   OVERALL

**Life is 10% what happens to us and 90%
how we react — Charles R. Swindoll**

Monday

Daily To Do

- [ ] Wake up & smile
- [ ] Walk/Run
- [ ] Gratitude
- [ ] Read
- [ ] Meditate
- [ ] Make Bed
- [ ] Donate
- [ ] Exercise
- [ ] Stretch
- [ ] Learn
- [ ] Thank you
- [ ] Day Prep
- [ ] Journal
- [ ] Visualize
- [ ] Water
- [ ] Water
- [ ] Water
- [ ] Go to sleep Happy!

Daily Calendar

5:00

6:00

7:00

8:00

9:00

10:00

11:00

12:00

1:00

2:00

3:00

4:00

5:00

6:00

7:00

8:00

9:00

Daily Focus

People to Contact

To Do Today

Gratitude

Personal
_____

Love & Relationships
_____

Professional
_____

Life
_____

#1 Priority to get me one step closer to achieving my main goal is:
_____

I am going to focus and improve on:
_____

Today is the first day of the rest of my beautiful life, what am I going to do to make a difference?
_____

Today is YOUR day and just by waking up it is already amazing!

Daily Reflection

Food Journal

Breakfast
Snack
Lunch
Snack
Dinner
Other

Exercise

RATE YOUR DAY

PERSONAL   LOVE   WORK   OVERALL

> What you think, you become. What you feel, you attract. What you imagine, you create. – Budda

Daily To Do

- [ ] Wake up & smile
- [ ] Walk/Run
- [ ] Gratitude
- [ ] Read
- [ ] Meditate
- [ ] Make Bed
- [ ] Donate
- [ ] Exercise
- [ ] Stretch
- [ ] Learn
- [ ] Thank you
- [ ] Day Prep
- [ ] Journal
- [ ] Visualize
- [ ] Water
- [ ] Water
- [ ] Water
- [ ] Go to sleep Happy!

Daily Calendar

5:00
6:00
7:00
8:00
9:00
10:00
11:00
12:00
1:00
2:00
3:00
4:00
5:00
6:00
7:00
8:00
9:00

Daily Focus

People to Contact

To Do Today

Gratitude

Personal

_____

Love & Relationships

_____

Professional

_____

Life

_____

#1 Priority to get me one step closer to achieving my main goal is:

_____

I am going to focus and improve on:

_____

Today is the first day of the rest of my beautiful life, what am I going to do to make a difference?

_____

Today is YOUR day and just by waking up it is already amazing!

Daily Reflection

Food Journal

Breakfast

Snack

Lunch

Snack

Dinner

Other

Exercise

RATE YOUR DAY

PERSONAL   LOVE   WORK   OVERALL

**Believe you CAN and you're already half
way there - Theodore Roosevelt**

Daily To Do

- ☐ Wake up & smile
- ☐ Walk/Run
- ☐ Gratitude
- ☐ Read
- ☐ Meditate
- ☐ Make Bed
- ☐ Donate
- ☐ Exercise
- ☐ Stretch
- ☐ Learn
- ☐ Thank you
- ☐ Day Prep
- ☐ Journal
- ☐ Visualize
- ☐ Water
- ☐ Water
- ☐ Water
- ☐ Go to sleep Happy!

Daily Calendar

5:00
6:00
7:00
8:00
9:00
10:00
11:00
12:00
1:00
2:00
3:00
4:00
5:00
6:00
7:00
8:00
9:00

Daily Focus

People to Contact

To Do Today

Gratitude

Personal
_____

Love & Relationships
_____

Professional
_____

Life
_____

#1 Priority to get me one step closer to achieving my main goal is:
_____

I am going to focus and improve on:
_____

Today is the first day of the rest of my beautiful life, what am I going to do to make a difference?
_____

Today is YOUR day
and just by waking up
it is already amazing!

Daily Reflection

Food Journal

Breakfast
Snack
Lunch
Snack
Dinner
Other

Exercise

RATE YOUR DAY

PERSONAL   LOVE   WORK   OVERALL

> The game of life is like the game of boomerangs; Our thoughts, words and actions return to us sooner or later and with astounding accuracy. – Florence Scovel Shinn

Daily To Do

- ☐ Wake up & smile
- ☐ Walk/Run
- ☐ Gratitude
- ☐ Read
- ☐ Meditate
- ☐ Make Bed
- ☐ Donate
- ☐ Exercise
- ☐ Stretch
- ☐ Learn
- ☐ Thank you
- ☐ Day Prep
- ☐ Journal
- ☐ Visualize
- ☐ Water
- ☐ Water
- ☐ Water
- ☐ Go to sleep Happy!

Daily Calendar

5:00
6:00
7:00
8:00
9:00
10:00
11:00
12:00
1:00
2:00
3:00
4:00
5:00
6:00
7:00
8:00
9:00

Daily Focus

People to Contact

To Do Today

Gratitude

Personal
_____

Love & Relationships
_____

Professional
_____

Life
_____

#1 Priority to get me one step closer to achieving my main goal is:
_____

I am going to focus and improve on:
_____

Today is the first day of the rest of my beautiful life, what am I going to do to make a difference?
_____

Daily Reflection
_____
_____
_____
_____
_____
_____
_____
_____
_____
_____
_____
_____

Food Journal

Breakfast
Snack
Lunch
Snack
Dinner
Other

Exercise

RATE YOUR DAY

PERSONAL   LOVE   WORK   OVERALL

Control your mind and you will control your world. – Norman Vincent Peale

Friday

Daily To Do

- [ ] Wake up & smile
- [ ] Walk/Run
- [ ] Gratitude
- [ ] Read
- [ ] Meditate
- [ ] Make Bed
- [ ] Donate
- [ ] Exercise
- [ ] Stretch
- [ ] Learn
- [ ] Thank you
- [ ] Day Prep
- [ ] Journal
- [ ] Visualize
- [ ] Water
- [ ] Water
- [ ] Water
- [ ] Go to sleep Happy!

Daily Calendar

5:00
6:00
7:00
8:00
9:00
10:00
11:00
12:00
1:00
2:00
3:00
4:00
5:00
6:00
7:00
8:00
9:00

Daily Focus

People to Contact

To Do Today

Gratitude

Personal
_____

Love & Relationships
_____

Professional
_____

Life
_____

#1 Priority to get me one step closer to achieving my main goal is:
_____

I am going to focus and improve on:
_____

Today is the first day of the rest of my beautiful life, what am I going to do to make a difference?
_____

Today is YOUR day
and just by waking up
it is already amazing!

Daily Reflection
_____
_____
_____
_____
_____
_____
_____
_____
_____
_____
_____
_____
_____
_____

Food Journal

Breakfast
Snack
Lunch
Snack
Dinner
Other

Exercise

RATE YOUR DAY

PERSONAL   LOVE   WORK   OVERALL

Your mind is a garden - Make sure to plant the ideas you want to grow

Daily To Do

- ☐ Wake up & smile
- ☐ Walk/Run
- ☐ Gratitude
- ☐ Read
- ☐ Meditate
- ☐ Make Bed
- ☐ Donate
- ☐ Exercise
- ☐ Stretch
- ☐ Learn
- ☐ Thank you
- ☐ Day Prep
- ☐ Journal
- ☐ Visualize
- ☐ Water
- ☐ Water
- ☐ Water
- ☐ Go to sleep Happy!

Daily Calendar

5:00

6:00

7:00

8:00

9:00

10:00

11:00

12:00

1:00

2:00

3:00

4:00

5:00

6:00

7:00

8:00

9:00

Daily Focus

People to Contact

To Do Today

Gratitude

Personal

_____

Love & Relationships

_____

Professional

_____

Life

_____

#1 Priority to get me one step closer to achieving my main goal is:

_____

I am going to focus and improve on:

_____

Today is the first day of the rest of my beautiful life, what am I going to do to make a difference?

_____

Daily Reflection

Food Journal

Breakfast

Snack

Lunch

Snack

Dinner

Other

Exercise

RATE YOUR DAY

PERSONAL   LOVE   WORK   OVERALL

Daily To Do

- [ ] Wake up & smile
- [ ] Walk/Run
- [ ] Gratitude
- [ ] Read
- [ ] Meditate
- [ ] Make Bed
- [ ] Donate
- [ ] Exercise
- [ ] Stretch
- [ ] Learn
- [ ] Thank you
- [ ] Day Prep
- [ ] Journal
- [ ] Visualize
- [ ] Water
- [ ] Water
- [ ] Water
- [ ] Go to sleep Happy!

Daily Calendar

5:00

6:00

7:00

8:00

9:00

10:00

11:00

12:00

1:00

2:00

3:00

4:00

5:00

6:00

7:00

8:00

9:00

Daily Focus

People to Contact

To Do Today

Sunday

Today is your day to relax, regroup, reflect and prepare for the next amazing week! What do you feel went really well this past week? List at least 5 accomplishments.

_____

_____

What would you like to improve on for this upcoming week?

_____

_____

What is ONE step that you will take this week to get closer to your dream?

_____

_____

Is there someone that could use your help this week? How can you make a difference?

_____

Weekly Challenge

Our mind believes ANYTHING that we repeatedly tell it! How powerful is that??

Your challenge this week is to create a personalized affirmation, write it out and tape it to your bathroom mirror. Then every time you go into the bathroom read it (out loud if possible). Read it, feel it, imagine it and smile.

Examples
I am beautiful, I am strong, I am sexy, I am in love, I am abundant, I am healthy,

I am grateful, I am wealthy, I am blessed.

I wake up every morning bursting with energy, excited to live my life to the fullest and CRUSH IT!!

Goals for this week

Health and Fitness

Love and Relationship

Career and Finance

Philanthropy and Giving Back

Shopping list

Hint:

Take a look at your one-year and three-month goals. How can you get closer to achieving them?

Gratitude

Personal
_____

Love & Relationships
_____

Professional
_____

Life
_____

#1 Priority to get me one step closer to achieving my main goal is:
_____

I am going to focus and improve on:
_____

Today is the first day of the rest of my beautiful life, what am I going to do to make a difference?
_____

Daily Reflection
_____
_____
_____
_____
_____
_____
_____
_____
_____
_____

Food Journal

Breakfast
Snack
Lunch
Snack
Dinner
Other

Exercise

RATE YOUR DAY

PERSONAL   LOVE   WORK   OVERALL

Being grateful for what you ALREADY have is by far the fastest way to attract more of what you want.

Daily To Do

- [ ] Wake up & smile
- [ ] Walk/Run
- [ ] Gratitude
- [ ] Read
- [ ] Meditate
- [ ] Make Bed
- [ ] Donate
- [ ] Exercise
- [ ] Stretch
- [ ] Learn
- [ ] Thank you
- [ ] Day Prep
- [ ] Journal
- [ ] Visualize
- [ ] Water
- [ ] Water
- [ ] Water
- [ ] Go to sleep Happy!

Daily Calendar

5:00

6:00

7:00

8:00

9:00

10:00

11:00

12:00

1:00

2:00

3:00

4:00

5:00

6:00

7:00

8:00

9:00

Daily Focus

People to Contact

To Do Today

Gratitude

Personal
_____

Love & Relationships
_____

Professional
_____

Life
_____

#1 Priority to get me one step closer to achieving my main goal is:
_____

I am going to focus and improve on:
_____

Today is the first day of the rest of my beautiful life, what am I going to do to make a difference?
_____

Daily Reflection

Food Journal

Breakfast _____
Snack _____
Lunch _____
Snack _____
Dinner _____
Other _____

Exercise

_____
_____

RATE YOUR DAY

PERSONAL   LOVE   WORK   OVERALL

Tuesday

Daily To Do

- ☐ Wake up & smile
- ☐ Walk/Run
- ☐ Gratitude
- ☐ Read
- ☐ Meditate
- ☐ Make Bed
- ☐ Donate
- ☐ Exercise
- ☐ Stretch
- ☐ Learn
- ☐ Thank you
- ☐ Day Prep
- ☐ Journal
- ☐ Visualize
- ☐ Water
- ☐ Water
- ☐ Water
- ☐ Go to sleep Happy!

Daily Calendar

5:00

6:00

7:00

8:00

9:00

10:00

11:00

12:00

1:00

2:00

3:00

4:00

5:00

6:00

7:00

8:00

9:00

Daily Focus

People to Contact

To Do Today

Gratitude

Personal
_____

Love & Relationships
_____

Professional
_____

Life
_____

#1 Priority to get me one step closer to achieving my main goal is:
_____

I am going to focus and improve on:
_____

Today is the first day of the rest of my beautiful life, what am I going to do to make a difference?
_____

Today is YOUR day and just by waking up it is already amazing!

Daily Reflection
_____
_____
_____
_____
_____
_____
_____
_____
_____
_____
_____
_____
_____

Food Journal

Breakfast
Snack
Lunch
Snack
Dinner
Other

Exercise

RATE YOUR DAY

PERSONAL   LOVE   WORK   OVERALL

Daily To Do

- [ ] Wake up & smile
- [ ] Walk/Run
- [ ] Gratitude
- [ ] Read
- [ ] Meditate
- [ ] Make Bed
- [ ] Donate
- [ ] Exercise
- [ ] Stretch
- [ ] Learn
- [ ] Thank you
- [ ] Day Prep
- [ ] Journal
- [ ] Visualize
- [ ] Water
- [ ] Water
- [ ] Water
- [ ] Go to sleep Happy!

Daily Calendar

5:00

6:00

7:00

8:00

9:00

10:00

11:00

12:00

1:00

2:00

3:00

4:00

5:00

6:00

7:00

8:00

9:00

Daily Focus

People to Contact

To Do Today

Gratitude

Personal
_____

Love & Relationships
_____

Professional
_____

Life
_____

#1 Priority to get me one step closer to achieving my main goal is:
_____

I am going to focus and improve on:
_____

Today is the first day of the rest of my beautiful life, what am I going to do to make a difference?
_____

Daily Reflection
_____
_____
_____
_____
_____
_____
_____
_____
_____
_____
_____

Food Journal

Breakfast
Snack
Lunch
Snack
Dinner
Other

Exercise

RATE YOUR DAY

PERSONAL   LOVE   WORK   OVERALL

Daily To Do

- ☐ Wake up & smile
- ☐ Walk/Run
- ☐ Gratitude
- ☐ Read
- ☐ Meditate
- ☐ Make Bed
- ☐ Donate
- ☐ Exercise
- ☐ Stretch
- ☐ Learn
- ☐ Thank you
- ☐ Day Prep
- ☐ Journal
- ☐ Visualize
- ☐ Water
- ☐ Water
- ☐ Water
- ☐ Go to sleep Happy!

Daily Calendar

5:00

6:00

7:00

8:00

9:00

10:00

11:00

12:00

1:00

2:00

3:00

4:00

5:00

6:00

7:00

8:00

9:00

Daily Focus

People to Contact

To Do Today

Gratitude

Personal
_____

Love & Relationships
_____

Professional
_____

Life
_____

#1 Priority to get me one step closer to achieving my main goal is:
_____

I am going to focus and improve on:
_____

Today is the first day of the rest of my beautiful life, what am I going to do to make a difference?
_____

Daily Reflection

Food Journal

Breakfast
Snack
Lunch
Snack
Dinner
Other

Exercise

RATE YOUR DAY

PERSONAL   LOVE   WORK   OVERALL

Daily To Do

- [ ] Wake up & smile
- [ ] Walk/Run
- [ ] Gratitude
- [ ] Read
- [ ] Meditate
- [ ] Make Bed
- [ ] Donate
- [ ] Exercise
- [ ] Stretch
- [ ] Learn
- [ ] Thank you
- [ ] Day Prep
- [ ] Journal
- [ ] Visualize
- [ ] Water
- [ ] Water
- [ ] Water
- [ ] Go to sleep Happy!

Daily Calendar

5:00

6:00

7:00

8:00

9:00

10:00

11:00

12:00

1:00

2:00

3:00

4:00

5:00

6:00

7:00

8:00

9:00

Daily Focus

People to Contact

To Do Today

Gratitude

Personal
_____

Love & Relationships
_____

Professional
_____

Life
_____

#1 Priority to get me one step closer to achieving my main goal is:
_____

I am going to focus and improve on:
_____

Today is the first day of the rest of my beautiful life, what am I going to do to make a difference?
_____

Today is YOUR day and just by waking up it is already amazing!

Daily Reflection
_____
_____
_____
_____
_____
_____
_____
_____
_____
_____
_____
_____
_____

Food Journal

Breakfast _____
Snack _____
Lunch _____
Snack _____
Dinner _____
Other _____

Exercise
_____
_____

RATE YOUR DAY

PERSONAL   LOVE   WORK   OVERALL

Daily To Do

- [ ] Wake up & smile
- [ ] Walk/Run
- [ ] Gratitude
- [ ] Read
- [ ] Meditate
- [ ] Make Bed
- [ ] Donate
- [ ] Exercise
- [ ] Stretch
- [ ] Learn
- [ ] Thank you
- [ ] Day Prep
- [ ] Journal
- [ ] Visualize
- [ ] Water
- [ ] Water
- [ ] Water
- [ ] Go to sleep Happy!

Daily Calendar

5:00

6:00

7:00

8:00

9:00

10:00

11:00

12:00

1:00

2:00

3:00

4:00

5:00

6:00

7:00

8:00

9:00

Daily Focus

People to Contact

To Do Today

Gratitude

Personal
_____

Love & Relationships
_____

Professional
_____

Life
_____

#1 Priority to get me one step closer to achieving my main goal is:
_____

I am going to focus and improve on:
_____

Today is the first day of the rest of my beautiful life, what am I going to do to make a difference?
_____

Daily Reflection
_____
_____
_____
_____
_____
_____
_____
_____
_____
_____
_____

Food Journal

Breakfast
Snack
Lunch
Snack
Dinner
Other

Exercise

RATE YOUR DAY

PERSONAL   LOVE   WORK   OVERALL

What you focus on, you become. –Frederick Lenz

Daily To Do

- [ ] Wake up & smile
- [ ] Walk/Run
- [ ] Gratitude
- [ ] Read
- [ ] Meditate
- [ ] Make Bed
- [ ] Donate
- [ ] Exercise
- [ ] Stretch
- [ ] Learn
- [ ] Thank you
- [ ] Day Prep
- [ ] Journal
- [ ] Visualize
- [ ] Water
- [ ] Water
- [ ] Water
- [ ] Go to sleep Happy!

Daily Calendar

5:00

6:00

7:00

8:00

9:00

10:00

11:00

12:00

1:00

2:00

3:00

4:00

5:00

6:00

7:00

8:00

9:00

Daily Focus

People to Contact

To Do Today

Sunday

Today is your day to relax, regroup, reflect and prepare for the next amazing week! What do you feel went really well this past week? List at least 5 accomplishments.

_____

_____

What would you like to improve on for this upcoming week?

_____

_____

What is ONE step that you will take this week to get closer to your dream?

_____

_____

Is there someone that could use your help this week? How can you make a difference?

_____

Weekly Challenge

The challenge this week is to be very mindful of your thoughts, words and actions. Make sure that you are thinking about what you WANT instead of what you do not want. Focus on everything wonderful that you want in your life instead of what you wish would go away. We attract what we think about, whether it's good or bad, so we might as well attract the things we desire.

Goals for this week

Health and Fitness

Love and Relationship

Career and Finance

Philanthropy and Giving Back

Shopping list

Hint:
Take a look at your one-year and three-month goals. How can you get closer to achieving them?

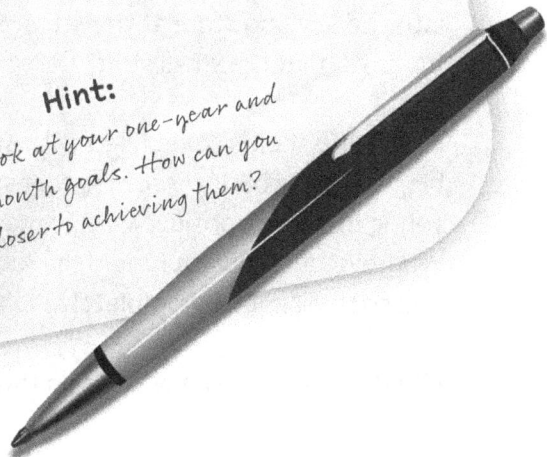

The Bigger Picture

Over the next two weeks, the focus is to look at the larger world outside of your own immediate circumstances. Sometimes it is easy to get caught up in the little details and annoyances that consume our mind but do not serve us. If this happens, take a step back, take a deep breath and look at the bigger picture.

When a situation starts to upset you or bring negative feelings into your life, decide if it is something that truly has a place in your day. If it is not something that is going to dramatically impact your (or your family's) future or safety, is it really worth getting upset about? Put each situation into perspective.

It is easy to let your day get thrown off-course by reacting when one little thing doesn't go your way. Try to keep your emotions in check; don't try to control every situation. The universal flow will always steer you in the best direction if you let it. There will be roadblocks and times when things don't go your way, but if you step back and try to see the lesson in the circumstance, it is usually the beginning to something better. Relax and go with the flow. Maintain keen awareness in every situation, trust your instincts and watch for life's guidance.

A really great way to put things into perspective is to lay outside on a warm, clear night, look up into the sky and stare at the stars. So much beauty and positivity to embrace—why waste time fussing about the small stuff?

If your life seems to be filled with small stuff then maybe it is time to get involved in something bigger. Join a charity or society that speaks to your heart, coach a kids' sports team and help develop young minds in a positive way, or maybe create your own club that works to create positive change. Whatever it is, get your mind thinking about greater things and the petty stuff will fall to the side and soon disappear completely.

Life is too great to be wasted on thoughts, deeds and words that don't feel good.

Book recommendations

The Four Agreements – Miguel Ruiz

The Celestine Prophecy – James Redfield

Don't Sweat the Small Stuff – Richard Carlson

Youtube Meditation

Meditation for Gaining Perspective and Seeing the Bigger Picture – Linda Hall

Affirmation

"In every situation – I choose to consider the Bigger Picture."

Gratitude

Personal
_____

Love & Relationships
_____

Professional
_____

Life
_____

#1 Priority to get me one step closer to achieving my main goal is:
_____

I am going to focus and improve on:
_____

Today is the first day of the rest of my beautiful life, what am I going to do to make a difference?
_____

Today is YOUR day and just by waking up it is already amazing!

Daily Reflection
_____
_____
_____
_____
_____
_____
_____
_____
_____
_____
_____

Food Journal

Breakfast
Snack
Lunch
Snack
Dinner
Other

Exercise

RATE YOUR DAY

PERSONAL   LOVE   WORK   OVERALL

Daily To Do

- [ ] Wake up & smile
- [ ] Walk/Run
- [ ] Gratitude
- [ ] Read
- [ ] Meditate
- [ ] Make Bed
- [ ] Donate
- [ ] Exercise
- [ ] Stretch
- [ ] Learn
- [ ] Thank you
- [ ] Day Prep
- [ ] Journal
- [ ] Visualize
- [ ] Water
- [ ] Water
- [ ] Water
- [ ] Go to sleep Happy!

Daily Calendar

5:00
6:00
7:00
8:00
9:00
10:00
11:00
12:00
1:00
2:00
3:00
4:00
5:00
6:00
7:00
8:00
9:00

Daily Focus

People to Contact

To Do Today

Gratitude

Personal
_____

Love & Relationships
_____

Professional
_____

Life
_____

#1 Priority to get me one step closer to achieving my main goal is:
_____

I am going to focus and improve on:
_____

Today is the first day of the rest of my beautiful life, what am I going to do to make a difference?
_____

Today is YOUR day
and just by waking up
it is already amazing!

Daily Reflection

Food Journal

Breakfast
Snack
Lunch
Snack
Dinner
Other

Exercise

RATE YOUR DAY

PERSONAL   LOVE   WORK   OVERALL

Daily To Do

- [ ] Wake up & smile
- [ ] Walk/Run
- [ ] Gratitude
- [ ] Read
- [ ] Meditate
- [ ] Make Bed
- [ ] Donate
- [ ] Exercise
- [ ] Stretch
- [ ] Learn
- [ ] Thank you
- [ ] Day Prep
- [ ] Journal
- [ ] Visualize
- [ ] Water
- [ ] Water
- [ ] Water
- [ ] Go to sleep Happy!

Daily Calendar

5:00

6:00

7:00

8:00

9:00

10:00

11:00

12:00

1:00

2:00

3:00

4:00

5:00

6:00

7:00

8:00

9:00

Daily Focus

People to Contact

To Do Today

Gratitude

Personal
_____

Love & Relationships
_____

Professional
_____

Life
_____

#1 Priority to get me one step closer to achieving my main goal is:
_____

I am going to focus and improve on:
_____

Today is the first day of the rest of my beautiful life, what am I going to do to make a difference?
_____

Today is YOUR day and just by waking up it is already amazing!

Daily Reflection

Food Journal

Breakfast
Snack
Lunch
Snack
Dinner
Other

Exercise

RATE YOUR DAY

PERSONAL   LOVE   WORK   OVERALL

> **Be happy in this moment, for this moment is your life. – Omar Khayyam**

Daily To Do

- ☐ Wake up & smile
- ☐ Walk/Run
- ☐ Gratitude
- ☐ Read
- ☐ Meditate
- ☐ Make Bed
- ☐ Donate
- ☐ Exercise
- ☐ Stretch
- ☐ Learn
- ☐ Thank you
- ☐ Day Prep
- ☐ Journal
- ☐ Visualize
- ☐ Water
- ☐ Water
- ☐ Water
- ☐ Go to sleep Happy!

Daily Calendar

5:00

6:00

7:00

8:00

9:00

10:00

11:00

12:00

1:00

2:00

3:00

4:00

5:00

6:00

7:00

8:00

9:00

Daily Focus

People to Contact

To Do Today

Gratitude

Personal
_____

Love & Relationships
_____

Professional
_____

Life
_____

#1 Priority to get me one step closer to achieving my main goal is:
_____

I am going to focus and improve on:
_____

Today is the first day of the rest of my beautiful life, what am I going to do to make a difference?
_____

Today is YOUR day and just by waking up it is already amazing!

Daily Reflection
_____
_____
_____
_____
_____
_____
_____
_____
_____
_____
_____
_____

Food Journal

Breakfast
Snack
Lunch
Snack
Dinner
Other

Exercise

RATE YOUR DAY

PERSONAL   LOVE   WORK   OVERALL

Daily To Do

- [ ] Wake up & smile
- [ ] Walk/Run
- [ ] Gratitude
- [ ] Read
- [ ] Meditate
- [ ] Make Bed
- [ ] Donate
- [ ] Exercise
- [ ] Stretch
- [ ] Learn
- [ ] Thank you
- [ ] Day Prep
- [ ] Journal
- [ ] Visualize
- [ ] Water
- [ ] Water
- [ ] Water
- [ ] Go to sleep Happy!

Daily Calendar

5:00

6:00

7:00

8:00

9:00

10:00

11:00

12:00

1:00

2:00

3:00

4:00

5:00

6:00

7:00

8:00

9:00

Daily Focus

People to Contact

To Do Today

Gratitude

Personal
_____

Love & Relationships
_____

Professional
_____

Life
_____

#1 Priority to get me one step closer to achieving my main goal is:
_____

I am going to focus and improve on:
_____

Today is the first day of the rest of my beautiful life, what am I going to do to make a difference?
_____

Daily Reflection
_____
_____
_____
_____
_____
_____
_____
_____
_____
_____

Food Journal

Breakfast
Snack
Lunch
Snack
Dinner
Other

Exercise

RATE YOUR DAY

PERSONAL   LOVE   WORK   OVERALL

Friday

Daily To Do

- [ ] Wake up & smile
- [ ] Walk/Run
- [ ] Gratitude
- [ ] Read
- [ ] Meditate
- [ ] Make Bed
- [ ] Donate
- [ ] Exercise
- [ ] Stretch
- [ ] Learn
- [ ] Thank you
- [ ] Day Prep
- [ ] Journal
- [ ] Visualize
- [ ] Water
- [ ] Water
- [ ] Water
- [ ] Go to sleep Happy!

Daily Calendar

5:00
6:00
7:00
8:00
9:00
10:00
11:00
12:00
1:00
2:00
3:00
4:00
5:00
6:00
7:00
8:00
9:00

Daily Focus

People to Contact

To Do Today

Gratitude

Personal
_____

Love & Relationships
_____

Professional
_____

Life
_____

#1 Priority to get me one step closer to achieving my main goal is:
_____

I am going to focus and improve on:
_____

Today is the first day of the rest of my beautiful life, what am I going to do to make a difference?
_____

Daily Reflection
_____
_____
_____
_____
_____
_____
_____
_____
_____
_____
_____
_____

Food Journal

Breakfast
Snack
Lunch
Snack
Dinner
Other

Exercise

RATE YOUR DAY

PERSONAL   LOVE   WORK   OVERALL

Daily To Do

- [ ] Wake up & smile
- [ ] Walk/Run
- [ ] Gratitude
- [ ] Read
- [ ] Meditate
- [ ] Make Bed
- [ ] Donate
- [ ] Exercise
- [ ] Stretch
- [ ] Learn
- [ ] Thank you
- [ ] Day Prep
- [ ] Journal
- [ ] Visualize
- [ ] Water
- [ ] Water
- [ ] Water
- [ ] Go to sleep Happy!

Daily Calendar

5:00
6:00
7:00
8:00
9:00
10:00
11:00
12:00
1:00
2:00
3:00
4:00
5:00
6:00
7:00
8:00
9:00

Daily Focus

People to Contact

To Do Today

Gratitude

Personal
_____

Love & Relationships
_____

Professional
_____

Life
_____

#1 Priority to get me one step closer to achieving my main goal is:
_____

I am going to focus and improve on:
_____

Today is the first day of the rest of my beautiful life, what am I going to do to make a difference?
_____

Today is YOUR day and just by waking up it is already amazing!

Daily Reflection
_____
_____
_____
_____
_____
_____
_____
_____
_____
_____
_____
_____

Food Journal

Breakfast
Snack
Lunch
Snack
Dinner
Other

Exercise

RATE YOUR DAY

PERSONAL   LOVE   WORK   OVERALL

Daily To Do

- [ ] Wake up & smile
- [ ] Walk/Run
- [ ] Gratitude
- [ ] Read
- [ ] Meditate
- [ ] Make Bed
- [ ] Donate
- [ ] Exercise
- [ ] Stretch
- [ ] Learn
- [ ] Thank you
- [ ] Day Prep
- [ ] Journal
- [ ] Visualize
- [ ] Water
- [ ] Water
- [ ] Water
- [ ] Go to sleep Happy!

Daily Calendar

5:00
6:00
7:00
8:00
9:00
10:00
11:00
12:00
1:00
2:00
3:00
4:00
5:00
6:00
7:00
8:00
9:00

Daily Focus

People to Contact

To Do Today

Sunday

Today is your day to relax, regroup, reflect and prepare for the next amazing week!
What do you feel went really well this past week? List at least 5 accomplishments.

_____

_____

What would you like to improve on for this upcoming week?

_____

_____

What is ONE step that you will take this week to get closer to your dream?

_____

_____

Is there someone that could use your help this week? How can you make a
difference?

_____

Weekly Challenge

Let's start some positive ripples in this world!

Whenever you are out and about this week (and even at home with your family) challenge yourself to smile at as many people as you can, hold the door open for people when
you have the chance and compliment people like crazy. You could change somebody's
whole day, maybe even their life!

Making other people feel good is scientifically proven to make you feel great. BONUS!

Goals for this week

Health and Fitness

Love and Relationship

Career and Finance

Philanthropy and Giving Back

Shopping list

Hint:
Take a look at your one-year and three-month goals. How can you get closer to achieving them?

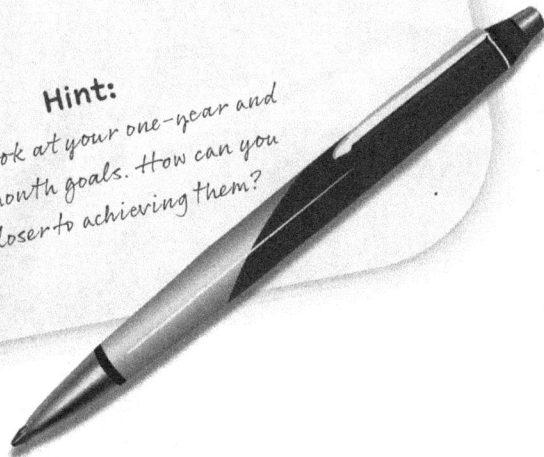

Gratitude

Personal

_____

Love & Relationships

_____

Professional

_____

Life

_____

#1 Priority to get me one step closer to achieving my main goal is:

_____

I am going to focus and improve on:

_____

Today is the first day of the rest of my beautiful life, what am I going to do to make a difference?

_____

Daily Reflection

_____
_____
_____
_____
_____
_____
_____
_____
_____

Food Journal

Breakfast
Snack
Lunch
Snack
Dinner
Other

Exercise

RATE YOUR DAY

PERSONAL   LOVE   WORK   OVERALL

> **If you don't like something change it! If you can't change it, change your attitude. – Maya Angelou**

Daily To Do

- ☐ Wake up & smile
- ☐ Walk/Run
- ☐ Gratitude
- ☐ Read
- ☐ Meditate
- ☐ Make Bed
- ☐ Donate
- ☐ Exercise
- ☐ Stretch
- ☐ Learn
- ☐ Thank you
- ☐ Day Prep
- ☐ Journal
- ☐ Visualize
- ☐ Water
- ☐ Water
- ☐ Water
- ☐ Go to sleep Happy!

Daily Calendar

5:00
6:00
7:00
8:00
9:00
10:00
11:00
12:00
1:00
2:00
3:00
4:00
5:00
6:00
7:00
8:00
9:00

Daily Focus

People to Contact

To Do Today

Gratitude

Personal
_____

Love & Relationships
_____

Professional
_____

Life
_____

#1 Priority to get me one step closer to achieving my main goal is:
_____

I am going to focus and improve on:
_____

Today is the first day of the rest of my beautiful life, what am I going to do to make a difference?
_____

Today is YOUR day
and just by waking up
it is already amazing!

Daily Reflection
_____
_____
_____
_____
_____
_____
_____
_____
_____
_____
_____
_____

Food Journal

Breakfast
Snack
Lunch
Snack
Dinner
Other

Exercise

RATE YOUR DAY

PERSONAL   LOVE   WORK   OVERALL

Daily To Do

- [ ] Wake up & smile
- [ ] Walk/Run
- [ ] Gratitude
- [ ] Read
- [ ] Meditate
- [ ] Make Bed
- [ ] Donate
- [ ] Exercise
- [ ] Stretch
- [ ] Learn
- [ ] Thank you
- [ ] Day Prep
- [ ] Journal
- [ ] Visualize
- [ ] Water
- [ ] Water
- [ ] Water
- [ ] Go to sleep Happy!

Daily Calendar

5:00

6:00

7:00

8:00

9:00

10:00

11:00

12:00

1:00

2:00

3:00

4:00

5:00

6:00

7:00

8:00

9:00

Daily Focus

People to Contact

To Do Today

Gratitude

Personal

_____

Love & Relationships

_____

Professional

_____

Life

_____

#1 Priority to get me one step closer to achieving my main goal is:

_____

I am going to focus and improve on:

_____

Today is the first day of the rest of my beautiful life, what am I going to do to make a difference?

_____

Daily Reflection

Food Journal

Breakfast
Snack
Lunch
Snack
Dinner
Other

Exercise

RATE YOUR DAY

PERSONAL   LOVE   WORK   OVERALL

Daily To Do

- [ ] Wake up & smile
- [ ] Walk/Run
- [ ] Gratitude
- [ ] Read
- [ ] Meditate
- [ ] Make Bed
- [ ] Donate
- [ ] Exercise
- [ ] Stretch
- [ ] Learn
- [ ] Thank you
- [ ] Day Prep
- [ ] Journal
- [ ] Visualize
- [ ] Water
- [ ] Water
- [ ] Water
- [ ] Go to sleep Happy!

Daily Calendar

5:00
6:00
7:00
8:00
9:00
10:00
11:00
12:00
1:00
2:00
3:00
4:00
5:00
6:00
7:00
8:00
9:00

Daily Focus

People to Contact

To Do Today

Gratitude

Personal

_____

Love & Relationships

_____

Professional

_____

Life

_____

#1 Priority to get me one step closer to achieving my main goal is:

_____

I am going to focus and improve on:

_____

Today is the first day of the rest of my beautiful life, what am I going to do to make a difference?

_____

Daily Reflection

_____
_____
_____
_____
_____
_____
_____
_____
_____
_____
_____

Food Journal

Breakfast

Snack

Lunch

Snack

Dinner

Other

Exercise

RATE YOUR DAY

PERSONAL   LOVE   WORK   OVERALL

Daily To Do

- [ ] Wake up & smile
- [ ] Walk/Run
- [ ] Gratitude
- [ ] Read
- [ ] Meditate
- [ ] Make Bed
- [ ] Donate
- [ ] Exercise
- [ ] Stretch
- [ ] Learn
- [ ] Thank you
- [ ] Day Prep
- [ ] Journal
- [ ] Visualize
- [ ] Water
- [ ] Water
- [ ] Water
- [ ] Go to sleep Happy!

Daily Calendar

5:00

6:00

7:00

8:00

9:00

10:00

11:00

12:00

1:00

2:00

3:00

4:00

5:00

6:00

7:00

8:00

9:00

Daily Focus

People to Contact

To Do Today

Gratitude

Personal
_____

Love & Relationships
_____

Professional
_____

Life
_____

#1 Priority to get me one step closer to achieving my main goal is:
_____

I am going to focus and improve on:
_____

Today is the first day of the rest of my beautiful life, what am I going to do to make a difference?
_____

Today is YOUR day and just by waking up it is already amazing!

Daily Reflection
_____
_____
_____
_____
_____
_____
_____
_____
_____
_____
_____
_____

Food Journal

Breakfast
Snack
Lunch
Snack
Dinner
Other

Exercise

RATE YOUR DAY

PERSONAL   LOVE   WORK   OVERALL

You have to dream before your dreams can come true. – APJ Abdul Kalam

Daily To Do

- [ ] Wake up & smile
- [ ] Walk/Run
- [ ] Gratitude
- [ ] Read
- [ ] Meditate
- [ ] Make Bed
- [ ] Donate
- [ ] Exercise
- [ ] Stretch
- [ ] Learn
- [ ] Thank you
- [ ] Day Prep
- [ ] Journal
- [ ] Visualize
- [ ] Water
- [ ] Water
- [ ] Water
- [ ] Go to sleep Happy!

Daily Calendar

5:00
6:00
7:00
8:00
9:00
10:00
11:00
12:00
1:00
2:00
3:00
4:00
5:00
6:00
7:00
8:00
9:00

Daily Focus

People to Contact

To Do Today

Gratitude

Personal
_____

Love & Relationships
_____

Professional
_____

Life
_____

#1 Priority to get me one step closer to achieving my main goal is:
_____

I am going to focus and improve on:
_____

Today is the first day of the rest of my beautiful life, what am I going to do to make a difference?
_____

Daily Reflection
_____
_____
_____
_____
_____
_____
_____
_____
_____
_____
_____
_____

Food Journal

Breakfast
Snack
Lunch
Snack
Dinner
Other

Exercise

RATE YOUR DAY

PERSONAL   LOVE   WORK   OVERALL

Daily To Do

- [ ] Wake up & smile
- [ ] Walk/Run
- [ ] Gratitude
- [ ] Read
- [ ] Meditate
- [ ] Make Bed
- [ ] Donate
- [ ] Exercise
- [ ] Stretch
- [ ] Learn
- [ ] Thank you
- [ ] Day Prep
- [ ] Journal
- [ ] Visualize
- [ ] Water
- [ ] Water
- [ ] Water
- [ ] Go to sleep Happy!

Daily Calendar

5:00

6:00

7:00

8:00

9:00

10:00

11:00

12:00

1:00

2:00

3:00

4:00

5:00

6:00

7:00

8:00

9:00

Daily Focus

People to Contact

To Do Today

Gratitude

Personal
_____

Love & Relationships
_____

Professional
_____

Life
_____

#1 Priority to get me one step closer to achieving my main goal is:
_____

I am going to focus and improve on:
_____

Today is the first day of the rest of my beautiful life, what am I going to do to make a difference?
_____

Daily Reflection

Food Journal

Breakfast
Snack
Lunch
Snack
Dinner
Other

Exercise

RATE YOUR DAY

PERSONAL   LOVE   WORK   OVERALL

Daily To Do

- ☐ Wake up & smile
- ☐ Walk/Run
- ☐ Gratitude
- ☐ Read
- ☐ Meditate
- ☐ Make Bed
- ☐ Donate
- ☐ Exercise
- ☐ Stretch
- ☐ Learn
- ☐ Thank you
- ☐ Day Prep
- ☐ Journal
- ☐ Visualize
- ☐ Water
- ☐ Water
- ☐ Water
- ☐ Go to sleep Happy!

Daily Calendar

5:00

6:00

7:00

8:00

9:00

10:00

11:00

12:00

1:00

2:00

3:00

4:00

5:00

6:00

7:00

8:00

9:00

Daily Focus

People to Contact

To Do Today

Sunday

Today is your day to relax, regroup, reflect and prepare for the next amazing week! What do you feel went really well this past week? List at least 5 accomplishments.

_____

_____

What would you like to improve on for this upcoming week?

_____

_____

What is ONE step that you will take this week to get closer to your dream?

_____

_____

Is there someone that could use your help this week? How can you make a difference?

_____

Weekly Challenge

Part of looking at the bigger picture of life is realizing and appreciating all the blessings that surround us every day. It is easy to get consumed by everyday tasks and begin living in our own little worlds, then start neglecting or unconsciously disregarding all the beautiful people, places and things that surround us. This can make life a little monotonous; let's brighten life up!

This week your challenge is to Google, 'Positive things happening in the world today,' or 'beautiful experiences.' Take some time to smile and enjoy stories of miracles that are happening all around us right now!

Does this light a fire inside of you to get involved? Maybe even bring one of your own ideas to life that will inspire or uplift the world!

Goals for this week

Health and Fitness

Love and Relationship

Career and Finance

Philanthropy and Giving Back

Shopping list

Hint:
Take a look at your one-year and three-month goals. How can you get closer to achieving them?

Fitness

We have all heard that exercise is healthy, it helps you live longer and makes you feel great … but did you know that exercise also has a huge impact on your ability to process information? Did you know that regular exercise can help control your mood, increase your energy levels, reduce stress, stimulate your mind to crave healthier food and can even positively affect your career and all-around success in life? And let's not forget the obvious benefits exercise provides of helping you look and feel your best. A great read on this is **The Mental Health Benefits of Exercise at** www.helpguide.org.

Exercise affects both your mind and your body in a positive way and in turn your good health will radiate out into a better life! The moment you decide to exercise on a steady basis and commit to a regular workout regimen, the better your life is going to be because a healthy mind and body will enable you to stay much more positive when life tries to kick your butt. So get out there and move that mass! You will notice rewards right away.

When you exercise, not only do you get your blood pumping (vital for getting oxygen to all your organs, keeping them healthy, happy and working hard for you) but you also release hormones called endorphins that have numerous positive impacts on your body—and a healthy body is crucial to having a healthy mind and soul!

Endorphins are natural 'feel good' chemicals. Endorphins act on the brain's pleasure receptors to improve your mood, which in turn will put a smile on your face, a little pep in your step and even help you sleep better. Endorphins make you feel good, can boost your confidence, reduce your stress levels and ultimately allow you to tackle more at work (and in life). This will lead to greater success in whatever you are trying to achieve. Powered by endorphins, you are able to take on bigger tasks and commitments and crush them because you have the energy, you have a clear mind, you are looking good, you are feeling confident and you are unstoppable!

Luckily for us, opportunities for exercise are pretty much unlimited. Most urban centres have gyms or recreation centres just about anyone can use. There are gyms just for women, 24-hour gyms, gyms with trainers, recreation centres featuring exercise classes and pools, yoga studios, spin gyms, martial arts academies, kick boxing classes, CrossFit training centres … There is a place for you to work out no matter your experience, budget or level of fitness.

If you are new to working out and want help learning proper techniques, there are trainers to be hired as well as unlimited online resources. If you work crazy hours and only have time to work out late at night or very early in the morning, find a 24-hour gym. If you have issues with your joints, look into Aqua fit classes at your local pool. There are also some amazing online gyms if you prefer to do your workout in the comfort of your own home. And if you're on a budget there are free workout videos on YouTube, anything from dance lessons and yoga to high intensity interval training (HIIT), stretching and muscle-specific workouts.

Or you could just start by getting outside for a walk, jog, run or hike. **The Positive Effects of Nature on Well Being: Evolutionary Biophilia** explains the added bonuses that fresh air and reconnecting with nature has on your mood, mind and creativity.

Book recommendation
Tone It Up: 28 Days to Fit, Fierce, and Fabulous – Karena & Katrina
Living the Good Life – Your guide to health and success – David Patchell

YouTube/Pinterest
Find any 30-day challenge, no matter what kind of workout it is—full body, arms, abs, booty—and take it on!

Affirmation
"I am strong. I am healthy, I am sexy. I am unstoppable in my workouts"

Gratitude

Personal

Love & Relationships

Professional

Life

#1 Priority to get me one step closer to achieving my main goal is:

I am going to focus and improve on:

Today is the first day of the rest of my beautiful life, what am I going to do to make a difference?

Daily Reflection

Food Journal

Breakfast

Snack

Lunch

Snack

Dinner

Other

Exercise

RATE YOUR DAY

PERSONAL   LOVE   WORK   OVERALL

Daily To Do

- [ ] Wake up & smile
- [ ] Walk/Run
- [ ] Gratitude
- [ ] Read
- [ ] Meditate
- [ ] Make Bed
- [ ] Donate
- [ ] Exercise
- [ ] Stretch
- [ ] Learn
- [ ] Thank you
- [ ] Day Prep
- [ ] Journal
- [ ] Visualize
- [ ] Water
- [ ] Water
- [ ] Water
- [ ] Go to sleep Happy!

Daily Calendar

5:00

6:00

7:00

8:00

9:00

10:00

11:00

12:00

1:00

2:00

3:00

4:00

5:00

6:00

7:00

8:00

9:00

Daily Focus

People to Contact

To Do Today

Gratitude

Personal
_____

Love & Relationships
_____

Professional
_____

Life
_____

#1 Priority to get me one step closer to achieving my main goal is:
_____

I am going to focus and improve on:
_____

Today is the first day of the rest of my beautiful life, what am I going to do to make a difference?
_____

Daily Reflection

Food Journal

Breakfast
Snack
Lunch
Snack
Dinner
Other

Exercise

RATE YOUR DAY

PERSONAL   LOVE   WORK   OVERALL

Daily To Do

- [ ] Wake up & smile
- [ ] Walk/Run
- [ ] Gratitude
- [ ] Read
- [ ] Meditate
- [ ] Make Bed
- [ ] Donate
- [ ] Exercise
- [ ] Stretch
- [ ] Learn
- [ ] Thank you
- [ ] Day Prep
- [ ] Journal
- [ ] Visualize
- [ ] Water
- [ ] Water
- [ ] Water
- [ ] Go to sleep Happy!

Daily Calendar

5:00

6:00

7:00

8:00

9:00

10:00

11:00

12:00

1:00

2:00

3:00

4:00

5:00

6:00

7:00

8:00

9:00

Daily Focus

People to Contact

To Do Today

Gratitude

Personal

_____

Love & Relationships

_____

Professional

_____

Life

_____

#1 Priority to get me one step closer to achieving my main goal is:

_____

I am going to focus and improve on:

_____

Today is the first day of the rest of my beautiful life, what am I going to do to make a difference?

_____

Today is YOUR day and just by waking up it is already amazing!

Daily Reflection

_____
_____
_____
_____
_____
_____
_____
_____
_____
_____
_____
_____

Food Journal

Breakfast

Snack

Lunch

Snack

Dinner

Other

Exercise

RATE YOUR DAY

PERSONAL   LOVE   WORK   OVERALL

Daily To Do

- ☐ Wake up & smile
- ☐ Walk/Run
- ☐ Gratitude
- ☐ Read
- ☐ Meditate
- ☐ Make Bed
- ☐ Donate
- ☐ Exercise
- ☐ Stretch
- ☐ Learn
- ☐ Thank you
- ☐ Day Prep
- ☐ Journal
- ☐ Visualize
- ☐ Water
- ☐ Water
- ☐ Water
- ☐ Go to sleep Happy!

Daily Calendar

5:00

6:00

7:00

8:00

9:00

10:00

11:00

12:00

1:00

2:00

3:00

4:00

5:00

6:00

7:00

8:00

9:00

Daily Focus

People to Contact

To Do Today

Gratitude

Personal
_____

Love & Relationships
_____

Professional
_____

Life
_____

#1 Priority to get me one step closer to achieving my main goal is:
_____

I am going to focus and improve on:
_____

Today is the first day of the rest of my beautiful life, what am I going to do to make a difference?
_____

Daily Reflection
_____
_____
_____
_____
_____
_____
_____
_____
_____
_____

Food Journal

Breakfast
Snack
Lunch
Snack
Dinner
Other

Exercise

RATE YOUR DAY

PERSONAL   LOVE   WORK   OVERALL

A good work out is when you make your dry fit shirt look like false advertising.

Daily To Do

- [ ] Wake up & smile
- [ ] Walk/Run
- [ ] Gratitude
- [ ] Read
- [ ] Meditate
- [ ] Make Bed
- [ ] Donate
- [ ] Exercise
- [ ] Stretch
- [ ] Learn
- [ ] Thank you
- [ ] Day Prep
- [ ] Journal
- [ ] Visualize
- [ ] Water
- [ ] Water
- [ ] Water
- [ ] Go to sleep Happy!

Daily Calendar

5:00

6:00

7:00

8:00

9:00

10:00

11:00

12:00

1:00

2:00

3:00

4:00

5:00

6:00

7:00

8:00

9:00

Daily Focus

People to Contact

To Do Today

Gratitude

Personal
_____

Love & Relationships
_____

Professional
_____

Life
_____

#1 Priority to get me one step closer to achieving my main goal is:
_____

I am going to focus and improve on:
_____

Today is the first day of the rest of my beautiful life, what am I going to do to make a difference?
_____

Today is YOUR day
and just by waking up
it is already amazing!

Daily Reflection
_____
_____
_____
_____
_____
_____
_____
_____
_____
_____
_____

Food Journal

Breakfast
Snack
Lunch
Snack
Dinner
Other

Exercise

RATE YOUR DAY

PERSONAL   LOVE   WORK   OVERALL

Sweat is magic. Cover yourself in it daily to grant all of your health wishes.

Daily To Do

- ☐ Wake up & smile
- ☐ Walk/Run
- ☐ Gratitude
- ☐ Read
- ☐ Meditate
- ☐ Make Bed
- ☐ Donate
- ☐ Exercise
- ☐ Stretch
- ☐ Learn
- ☐ Thank you
- ☐ Day Prep
- ☐ Journal
- ☐ Visualize
- ☐ Water
- ☐ Water
- ☐ Water
- ☐ Go to sleep Happy!

Daily Calendar

5:00
6:00
7:00
8:00
9:00
10:00
11:00
12:00
1:00
2:00
3:00
4:00
5:00
6:00
7:00
8:00
9:00

Daily Focus

People to Contact

To Do Today

Gratitude

Personal
_____

Love & Relationships
_____

Professional
_____

Life
_____

#1 Priority to get me one step closer to achieving my main goal is:
_____

I am going to focus and improve on:
_____

Today is the first day of the rest of my beautiful life, what am I going to do to make a difference?
_____

Daily Reflection

Food Journal

Breakfast _____
Snack _____
Lunch _____
Snack _____
Dinner _____
Other _____

Exercise
_____
_____

RATE YOUR DAY

PERSONAL   LOVE   WORK   OVERALL

You can feel SORE tomorrow, or you can feel SORRY. You choose!

Saturday

Daily To Do

- [ ] Wake up & smile
- [ ] Walk/Run
- [ ] Gratitude
- [ ] Read
- [ ] Meditate
- [ ] Make Bed
- [ ] Donate
- [ ] Exercise
- [ ] Stretch
- [ ] Learn
- [ ] Thank you
- [ ] Day Prep
- [ ] Journal
- [ ] Visualize
- [ ] Water
- [ ] Water
- [ ] Water
- [ ] Go to sleep Happy!

Daily Calendar

5:00
6:00
7:00
8:00
9:00
10:00
11:00
12:00
1:00
2:00
3:00
4:00
5:00
6:00
7:00
8:00
9:00

Daily Focus

People to Contact

To Do Today

Gratitude

Personal

_____

Love & Relationships

_____

Professional

_____

Life

_____

#1 Priority to get me one step closer to achieving my main goal is:

_____

I am going to focus and improve on:

_____

Today is the first day of the rest of my beautiful life, what am I going to do to make a difference?

_____

Daily Reflection

_____
_____
_____
_____
_____
_____
_____
_____
_____
_____
_____
_____

Food Journal

Breakfast

Snack

Lunch

Snack

Dinner

Other

Exercise

RATE YOUR DAY

PERSONAL   LOVE   WORK   OVERALL

Think of your workouts as important meetings you've scheduled with yourself - BOSSES don't cancel - Cristina Carlyle

Sunday

Daily To Do

- ☐ Wake up & smile
- ☐ Walk/Run
- ☐ Gratitude
- ☐ Read
- ☐ Meditate
- ☐ Make Bed
- ☐ Donate
- ☐ Exercise
- ☐ Stretch
- ☐ Learn
- ☐ Thank you
- ☐ Day Prep
- ☐ Journal
- ☐ Visualize
- ☐ Water
- ☐ Water
- ☐ Water
- ☐ Go to sleep Happy!

Daily Calendar

5:00

6:00

7:00

8:00

9:00

10:00

11:00

12:00

1:00

2:00

3:00

4:00

5:00

6:00

7:00

8:00

9:00

Daily Focus

People to Contact

To Do Today

Sunday

Today is your day to relax, regroup, reflect and prepare for the next amazing week! What do you feel went really well this past week? List at least 5 accomplishments.

_____

_____

What would you like to improve on for this upcoming week?

_____

_____

What is ONE step that you will take this week to get closer to your dream?

_____

_____

Is there someone that could use your help this week? How can you make a difference?

_____

Weekly Challenge

Your challenge this week is to try a new fitness class!

Bring a buddy or try it solo, it doesn't matter — just do it!

* Yoga   * Boxing

* Dance   * TRX

*Aerobics   * Spin

Anything at all! Just try something new!

Goals for this week

Health and Fitness

Love and Relationship

Career and Finance

Philanthropy and Giving Back

Hint:
Take a look at your one-year and three-month goals. How can you get closer to achieving them?

Shopping list

Gratitude

Personal
_____

Love & Relationships
_____

Professional
_____

Life
_____

#1 Priority to get me one step closer to achieving my main goal is:
_____

I am going to focus and improve on:
_____

Today is the first day of the rest of my beautiful life, what am I going to do to make a difference?
_____

Daily Reflection

_____
_____
_____
_____
_____
_____
_____
_____
_____

Food Journal

Breakfast
Snack
Lunch
Snack
Dinner
Other

Exercise

RATE YOUR DAY

PERSONAL   LOVE   WORK   OVERALL

The BODY achieves what the MIND believes

Monday

Daily To Do

- ☐ Wake up & smile
- ☐ Walk/Run
- ☐ Gratitude
- ☐ Read
- ☐ Meditate
- ☐ Make Bed
- ☐ Donate
- ☐ Exercise
- ☐ Stretch
- ☐ Learn
- ☐ Thank you
- ☐ Day Prep
- ☐ Journal
- ☐ Visualize
- ☐ Water
- ☐ Water
- ☐ Water
- ☐ Go to sleep Happy!

Daily Calendar

- 5:00
- 6:00
- 7:00
- 8:00
- 9:00
- 10:00
- 11:00
- 12:00
- 1:00
- 2:00
- 3:00
- 4:00
- 5:00
- 6:00
- 7:00
- 8:00
- 9:00

Daily Focus

People to Contact

To Do Today

Gratitude

Personal

_____

Love & Relationships

_____

Professional

_____

Life

_____

#1 Priority to get me one step closer to achieving my main goal is:

_____

I am going to focus and improve on:

_____

Today is the first day of the rest of my beautiful life, what am I going to do to make a difference?

_____

Daily Reflection

_____
_____
_____
_____
_____
_____
_____
_____
_____
_____
_____

Food Journal

Breakfast

Snack

Lunch

Snack

Dinner

Other

Exercise

RATE YOUR DAY

PERSONAL   LOVE   WORK   OVERALL

Every day is a chance to get stronger, eat better, live healthier and to be the very best version of YOU. - G Kemle

Daily To Do

- [ ] Wake up & smile
- [ ] Walk/Run
- [ ] Gratitude
- [ ] Read
- [ ] Meditate
- [ ] Make Bed
- [ ] Donate
- [ ] Exercise
- [ ] Stretch
- [ ] Learn
- [ ] Thank you
- [ ] Day Prep
- [ ] Journal
- [ ] Visualize
- [ ] Water
- [ ] Water
- [ ] Water
- [ ] Go to sleep Happy!

Daily Calendar

5:00

6:00

7:00

8:00

9:00

10:00

11:00

12:00

1:00

2:00

3:00

4:00

5:00

6:00

7:00

8:00

9:00

Daily Focus

People to Contact

To Do Today

Gratitude

Personal
_____

Love & Relationships
_____

Professional
_____

Life
_____

#1 Priority to get me one step closer to achieving my main goal is:
_____

I am going to focus and improve on:
_____

Today is the first day of the rest of my beautiful life, what am I going to do to make a difference?
_____

Daily Reflection
_____
_____
_____
_____
_____
_____
_____
_____
_____
_____

Food Journal

Breakfast
Snack
Lunch
Snack
Dinner
Other

Exercise

RATE YOUR DAY

PERSONAL   LOVE   WORK   OVERALL

Daily To Do

- [ ] Wake up & smile
- [ ] Walk/Run
- [ ] Gratitude
- [ ] Read
- [ ] Meditate
- [ ] Make Bed
- [ ] Donate
- [ ] Exercise
- [ ] Stretch
- [ ] Learn
- [ ] Thank you
- [ ] Day Prep
- [ ] Journal
- [ ] Visualize
- [ ] Water
- [ ] Water
- [ ] Water
- [ ] Go to sleep Happy!

Daily Calendar

5:00

6:00

7:00

8:00

9:00

10:00

11:00

12:00

1:00

2:00

3:00

4:00

5:00

6:00

7:00

8:00

9:00

Daily Focus

People to Contact

To Do Today

Gratitude

Personal
_____

Love & Relationships
_____

Professional
_____

Life
_____

#1 Priority to get me one step closer to achieving my main goal is:
_____

I am going to focus and improve on:
_____

Today is the first day of the rest of my beautiful life, what am I going to do to make a difference?
_____

Today is YOUR day
and just by waking up
it is already amazing!

Daily Reflection
_____
_____
_____
_____
_____
_____
_____
_____
_____
_____
_____
_____

Food Journal

Breakfast
Snack
Lunch
Snack
Dinner
Other

Exercise

RATE YOUR DAY

PERSONAL   LOVE   WORK   OVERALL

Pain is just weakness leaving the body

Thursday

Daily To Do

- [ ] Wake up & smile
- [ ] Walk/Run
- [ ] Gratitude
- [ ] Read
- [ ] Meditate
- [ ] Make Bed
- [ ] Donate
- [ ] Exercise
- [ ] Stretch
- [ ] Learn
- [ ] Thank you
- [ ] Day Prep
- [ ] Journal
- [ ] Visualize
- [ ] Water
- [ ] Water
- [ ] Water
- [ ] Go to sleep Happy!

Daily Calendar

5:00
6:00
7:00
8:00
9:00
10:00
11:00
12:00
1:00
2:00
3:00
4:00
5:00
6:00
7:00
8:00
9:00

Daily Focus

People to Contact

To Do Today

Gratitude

Personal
_____

Love & Relationships
_____

Professional
_____

Life
_____

#1 Priority to get me one step closer to achieving my main goal is:
_____

I am going to focus and improve on:
_____

Today is the first day of the rest of my beautiful life, what am I going to do to make a difference?
_____

Daily Reflection

_____
_____
_____
_____
_____
_____
_____
_____
_____
_____

Food Journal

Breakfast
Snack
Lunch
Snack
Dinner
Other

Exercise

RATE YOUR DAY

PERSONAL   LOVE   WORK   OVERALL

Daily To Do

- ☐ Wake up & smile
- ☐ Walk/Run
- ☐ Gratitude
- ☐ Read
- ☐ Meditate
- ☐ Make Bed
- ☐ Donate
- ☐ Exercise
- ☐ Stretch
- ☐ Learn
- ☐ Thank you
- ☐ Day Prep
- ☐ Journal
- ☐ Visualize
- ☐ Water
- ☐ Water
- ☐ Water
- ☐ Go to sleep Happy!

Daily Calendar

5:00

6:00

7:00

8:00

9:00

10:00

11:00

12:00

1:00

2:00

3:00

4:00

5:00

6:00

7:00

8:00

9:00

Daily Focus

People to Contact

To Do Today

Gratitude

Personal
_____

Love & Relationships
_____

Professional
_____

Life
_____

#1 Priority to get me one step closer to achieving my main goal is:
_____

I am going to focus and improve on:
_____

Today is the first day of the rest of my beautiful life, what am I going to do to make a difference?
_____

Daily Reflection

Food Journal

Breakfast
Snack
Lunch
Snack
Dinner
Other

Exercise

RATE YOUR DAY

PERSONAL   LOVE   WORK   OVERALL

Daily To Do

- [ ] Wake up & smile
- [ ] Walk/Run
- [ ] Gratitude
- [ ] Read
- [ ] Meditate
- [ ] Make Bed
- [ ] Donate
- [ ] Exercise
- [ ] Stretch
- [ ] Learn
- [ ] Thank you
- [ ] Day Prep
- [ ] Journal
- [ ] Visualize
- [ ] Water
- [ ] Water
- [ ] Water
- [ ] Go to sleep Happy!

Daily Calendar

5:00

6:00

7:00

8:00

9:00

10:00

11:00

12:00

1:00

2:00

3:00

4:00

5:00

6:00

7:00

8:00

9:00

Daily Focus

People to Contact

To Do Today

Gratitude

Personal

_____

Love & Relationships

_____

Professional

_____

Life

_____

#1 Priority to get me one step closer to achieving my main goal is:

_____

I am going to focus and improve on:

_____

Today is the first day of the rest of my beautiful life, what am I going to do to make a difference?

_____

Today is YOUR day
and just by waking up
it is already amazing!

Daily Reflection

_____
_____
_____
_____
_____
_____
_____
_____
_____
_____
_____
_____

Food Journal

Breakfast

Snack

Lunch

Snack

Dinner

Other

Exercise

RATE YOUR DAY

PERSONAL   LOVE   WORK   OVERALL

Daily To Do

- [ ] Wake up & smile
- [ ] Walk/Run
- [ ] Gratitude
- [ ] Read
- [ ] Meditate
- [ ] Make Bed
- [ ] Donate
- [ ] Exercise
- [ ] Stretch
- [ ] Learn
- [ ] Thank you
- [ ] Day Prep
- [ ] Journal
- [ ] Visualize
- [ ] Water
- [ ] Water
- [ ] Water
- [ ] Go to sleep Happy!

Daily Calendar

5:00

6:00

7:00

8:00

9:00

10:00

11:00

12:00

1:00

2:00

3:00

4:00

5:00

6:00

7:00

8:00

9:00

Daily Focus

People to Contact

To Do Today

Sunday

Today is your day to relax, regroup, reflect and prepare for the next amazing week! What do you feel went really well this past week? List at least 5 accomplishments.

_____

_____

What would you like to improve on for this upcoming week?

_____

_____

What is ONE step that you will take this week to get closer to your dream?

_____

_____

Is there someone that could use your help this week? How can you make a difference?

_____

Weekly Challenge

Big challenges produce big advances, big dreams create big success, with big steps comes big achievement.

The challenge this week is to register for something BIG. How about a race — a 5-kilometre, 10-kilometre or half-marathon ... or maybe even a marathon! Or if you're really ambitious, how about registering for a triathlon, Tough Mudder or Iron man competition?

Anything that requires physical training will do; just be sure to take the appropriate steps to prepare for it. Consult a physician and condition yourself properly for whatever event you choose to tackle, then get some like-minded friends, train hard, push your boundaries and feel that unreal feeling of achievement.

Goals for this week

Health and Fitness

Love and Relationship

Career and Finance

Philanthropy and Giving Back

Shopping list

Hint:
Take a look at your one-year and three-month goals. How can you get closer to achieving them?

Nutrition

You have complete control over something that affects your entire life—what you put in your mouth. Nutrition affects how much energy you have, your mood, how you sleep, the way you feel on the inside and how you look on the outside. Your nutritional health directly correlates with how you perform at work, school, sports and basically everything else in life that requires you to move or think.

All our bodies and dietary needs are different, so it is definitely worth taking a little time to figure out exactly what makes your body thrive. Once you figure out your needs and start fueling your body, instead of just filling it, I guarantee your whole world will change.

Your body is incredibly smart; it tells you exactly what you need and when you need it—you just have to learn how to listen to it. You know when you feel an afternoon slump and get super moody? Either you're hungry or, if you just ate a quick snack packaged in plastic, then your body may be looking for actual nutrition.

Be mindful when preparing your food, be present when choosing your food and really taste your food when you're chewing it (and be sure to chew it like crazy). I remember my grandpa would set his utensils down after every bite he put in his mouth and then he would chew for what felt like an eternity! I never understood why he did that, because I was filling up my next spoonful before I had even swallowed! I just couldn't wait to get the next bite in there. But after several years I figured out what a smart man he was. Your mouth is where all your taste buds are; that's where the pleasure of eating takes place … that is where the magic happens! Chewing your food *properly* releases majority of the nutrients and the more we chew our food, the less our intestines have to work.

Give your organs a break and get the most out of your food—CHEW!

Obviously, choosing healthy, fresh, colourful and local foods whenever possible is best, but when you have a cheat meal, enjoy it! Overindulging on foods that are not beneficial to your health is how people get into nutritional trouble. Take time and be mindful when you're having special treats (whether it's a nice glass of wine, an ice cream cone or nachos on game day). Studies have shown that feeling guilty about cheat meals or snacks actually increases the desire to eat those things, so just savor your food—really taste it—then get back to the fruits, veggies and water.

Remember how I said your body is incredibly smart and that you just have to learn to listen to it? Have you ever had a hangover? That is your body begging you to stop poisoning it.

Drugs and alcohol may temporarily make you feel invincible, however the moment the expensive rush is over you are likely to be two or three times lower in energy then you were before you started your bender. The harm you cause, to not only your body but also to your mind and soul, can take years off your life—and you have a special gift to share with the world so we need you here as long as possible!

The good news is that you can get the same high with NO negative side effects through meditation, extreme sports, running, exercise, funny movies and sex! All of these things are awesome options that leave you feeling good a lot longer than any drug or alcohol and cost far less as well. Try one of those out next time you feel the need to escape.

HUGE nutrition tip – Drink water, water, water and some more water. Water aids in digestion, regulates your temperature, protects your cells, joints and spinal cord and makes up approximately 70 percent of you—your cells and body! Water is a super important part of our diet!

To get the best nutrition, small changes can make a huge difference. Try to incorporate some of these small changes into your life:

- Weekly meal preparation—this is huge for me. Life gets busy, but if you have already taken a couple of hours on a Sunday to shop, chop and prepare healthy, fresh, delicious foods the better your week is going to go and the better you are going to feel!
- When going shopping for groceries at your local farmers market (if possible) or the grocery store, make sure you eat before you go! That way, you won't be tempted to buy inappropriate foods.
- Stick to the perimeter of the store; the fruits and veggies, meat and dairy are all on the outside while the middle isles contain mostly processed and packaged foods, which are best to stay away from.
- Meatless Mondays!
- Try to make sure your plate is half-full of fresh vegetables and/or fruits.

Books
Joyous Health – Joy McCarthy
28 days to a Fit Fierce and Fabulous YOU – Tone It Up

Youtube/Pinterest
Delicious vegetarian meals – Go crazy!

Affirmation
"I eat food to fuel and nourish my mind, body and soul"

Gratitude

Personal
_____

Love & Relationships
_____

Professional
_____

Life
_____

#1 Priority to get me one step closer to achieving my main goal is:
_____

I am going to focus and improve on:
_____

Today is the first day of the rest of my beautiful life, what am I going to do to make a difference?
_____

Daily Reflection
_____
_____
_____
_____
_____
_____
_____
_____
_____
_____

Food Journal

Breakfast
Snack
Lunch
Snack
Dinner
Other

Exercise

RATE YOUR DAY

PERSONAL   LOVE   WORK   OVERALL

Anyone can work out for an hour, but to control what you put on your plate the other 23 hours - now that is strength!

Monday

Daily To Do

- [ ] Wake up & smile
- [ ] Walk/Run
- [ ] Gratitude
- [ ] Read
- [ ] Meditate
- [ ] Make Bed
- [ ] Donate
- [ ] Exercise
- [ ] Stretch
- [ ] Learn
- [ ] Thank you
- [ ] Day Prep
- [ ] Journal
- [ ] Visualize
- [ ] Water
- [ ] Water
- [ ] Water
- [ ] Go to sleep Happy!

Daily Calendar

5:00
6:00
7:00
8:00
9:00
10:00
11:00
12:00
1:00
2:00
3:00
4:00
5:00
6:00
7:00
8:00
9:00

Daily Focus

People to Contact

To Do Today

Gratitude

Personal
_____

Love & Relationships
_____

Professional
_____

Life
_____

#1 Priority to get me one step closer to achieving my main goal is:
_____

I am going to focus and improve on:
_____

Today is the first day of the rest of my beautiful life, what am I going to do to make a difference?
_____

Daily Reflection

Food Journal

Breakfast
Snack
Lunch
Snack
Dinner
Other

Exercise

RATE YOUR DAY

PERSONAL   LOVE   WORK   OVERALL

Eat healthy - BE healthy.

Tuesday

Daily To Do

- [ ] Wake up & smile
- [ ] Walk/Run
- [ ] Gratitude
- [ ] Read
- [ ] Meditate
- [ ] Make Bed
- [ ] Donate
- [ ] Exercise
- [ ] Stretch
- [ ] Learn
- [ ] Thank you
- [ ] Day Prep
- [ ] Journal
- [ ] Visualize
- [ ] Water
- [ ] Water
- [ ] Water
- [ ] Go to sleep Happy!

Daily Calendar

5:00

6:00

7:00

8:00

9:00

10:00

11:00

12:00

1:00

2:00

3:00

4:00

5:00

6:00

7:00

8:00

9:00

Daily Focus

People to Contact

To Do Today

Gratitude

Personal
_____

Love & Relationships
_____

Professional
_____

Life
_____

#1 Priority to get me one step closer to achieving my main goal is:
_____

I am going to focus and improve on:
_____

Today is the first day of the rest of my beautiful life, what am I going to do to make a difference?
_____

Today is YOUR day and just by waking up it is already amazing!

Daily Reflection
_____
_____
_____
_____
_____
_____
_____
_____
_____
_____

Food Journal

Breakfast
Snack
Lunch
Snack
Dinner
Other

Exercise

RATE YOUR DAY

PERSONAL   LOVE   WORK   OVERALL

Health is much more dependent on our habits and nutrition than on medicine. – John Lubbock

Wednesday

Daily To Do

- [ ] Wake up & smile
- [ ] Walk/Run
- [ ] Gratitude
- [ ] Read
- [ ] Meditate
- [ ] Make Bed
- [ ] Donate
- [ ] Exercise
- [ ] Stretch
- [ ] Learn
- [ ] Thank you
- [ ] Day Prep
- [ ] Journal
- [ ] Visualize
- [ ] Water
- [ ] Water
- [ ] Water
- [ ] Go to sleep Happy!

Daily Calendar

5:00

6:00

7:00

8:00

9:00

10:00

11:00

12:00

1:00

2:00

3:00

4:00

5:00

6:00

7:00

8:00

9:00

Daily Focus

People to Contact

To Do Today

Gratitude

Personal
_____

Love & Relationships
_____

Professional
_____

Life
_____

#1 Priority to get me one step closer to achieving my main goal is:
_____

I am going to focus and improve on:
_____

Today is the first day of the rest of my beautiful life, what am I going to do to make a difference?
_____

Daily Reflection
_____
_____
_____
_____
_____
_____
_____
_____
_____
_____
_____

Food Journal

Breakfast _____
Snack _____
Lunch _____
Snack _____
Dinner _____
Other _____

Exercise
_____
_____

RATE YOUR DAY

PERSONAL   LOVE   WORK   OVERALL

> The way you think, the way you behave, the way you eat can influence your life by 30 to 50 years! – Deepak Chopra

Daily To Do

- [ ] Wake up & smile
- [ ] Walk/Run
- [ ] Gratitude
- [ ] Read
- [ ] Meditate
- [ ] Make Bed
- [ ] Donate
- [ ] Exercise
- [ ] Stretch
- [ ] Learn
- [ ] Thank you
- [ ] Day Prep
- [ ] Journal
- [ ] Visualize
- [ ] Water
- [ ] Water
- [ ] Water
- [ ] Go to sleep Happy!

Daily Calendar

5:00
6:00
7:00
8:00
9:00
10:00
11:00
12:00
1:00
2:00
3:00
4:00
5:00
6:00
7:00
8:00
9:00

Daily Focus

People to Contact

To Do Today

Gratitude

Personal
_____

Love & Relationships
_____

Professional
_____

Life
_____

#1 Priority to get me one step closer to achieving my main goal is:
_____

I am going to focus and improve on:
_____

Today is the first day of the rest of my beautiful life, what am I going to do to make a difference?
_____

Daily Reflection

Food Journal

Breakfast

Snack

Lunch

Snack

Dinner

Other

Exercise

RATE YOUR DAY

PERSONAL   LOVE   WORK   OVERALL

Daily To Do

- [ ] Wake up & smile
- [ ] Walk/Run
- [ ] Gratitude
- [ ] Read
- [ ] Meditate
- [ ] Make Bed
- [ ] Donate
- [ ] Exercise
- [ ] Stretch
- [ ] Learn
- [ ] Thank you
- [ ] Day Prep
- [ ] Journal
- [ ] Visualize
- [ ] Water
- [ ] Water
- [ ] Water
- [ ] Go to sleep Happy!

Daily Calendar

5:00
6:00
7:00
8:00
9:00
10:00
11:00
12:00
1:00
2:00
3:00
4:00
5:00
6:00
7:00
8:00
9:00

Daily Focus

People to Contact

To Do Today

Gratitude

Personal
_____

Love & Relationships
_____

Professional
_____

Life
_____

#1 Priority to get me one step closer to achieving my main goal is:
_____

I am going to focus and improve on:
_____

Today is the first day of the rest of my beautiful life, what am I going to do to make a difference?
_____

Daily Reflection
_____
_____
_____
_____
_____
_____
_____
_____
_____
_____
_____
_____
_____

Food Journal

Breakfast
Snack
Lunch
Snack
Dinner
Other

Exercise

RATE YOUR DAY

PERSONAL   LOVE   WORK   OVERALL

They say " you are what you eat" That's funny. I don't remember you eating a sexy beast this morning;)

Saturday

Daily To Do

- [ ] Wake up & smile
- [ ] Walk/Run
- [ ] Gratitude
- [ ] Read
- [ ] Meditate
- [ ] Make Bed
- [ ] Donate
- [ ] Exercise
- [ ] Stretch
- [ ] Learn
- [ ] Thank you
- [ ] Day Prep
- [ ] Journal
- [ ] Visualize
- [ ] Water
- [ ] Water
- [ ] Water
- [ ] Go to sleep Happy!

Daily Calendar

5:00

6:00

7:00

8:00

9:00

10:00

11:00

12:00

1:00

2:00

3:00

4:00

5:00

6:00

7:00

8:00

9:00

Daily Focus

People to Contact

To Do Today

Gratitude

Personal

_____

Love & Relationships

_____

Professional

_____

Life

_____

#1 Priority to get me one step closer to achieving my main goal is:

_____

I am going to focus and improve on:

_____

Today is the first day of the rest of my beautiful life, what am I going to do to make a difference?

_____

Daily Reflection

Food Journal

Breakfast
Snack
Lunch
Snack
Dinner
Other

Exercise

RATE YOUR DAY

PERSONAL   LOVE   WORK   OVERALL

Daily To Do

- [ ] Wake up & smile
- [ ] Walk/Run
- [ ] Gratitude
- [ ] Read
- [ ] Meditate
- [ ] Make Bed
- [ ] Donate
- [ ] Exercise
- [ ] Stretch
- [ ] Learn
- [ ] Thank you
- [ ] Day Prep
- [ ] Journal
- [ ] Visualize
- [ ] Water
- [ ] Water
- [ ] Water
- [ ] Go to sleep Happy!

Daily Calendar

5:00
6:00
7:00
8:00
9:00
10:00
11:00
12:00
1:00
2:00
3:00
4:00
5:00
6:00
7:00
8:00
9:00

Daily Focus

People to Contact

To Do Today

Sunday

Today is your day to relax, regroup, reflect and prepare for the next amazing week!
What do you feel went really well this past week? List at least 5 accomplishments.

_____

_____

What would you like to improve on for this upcoming week?

_____

_____

What is ONE step that you will take this week to get closer to your dream?

_____

_____

Is there someone that could use your help this week? How can you make a difference?

_____

Weekly Challenge

Hydrate, H_2O! Hydrate, H_2O! Do you know how crucial water is for our planet? Without it, every living thing would die. So think about how important it is for you! Water hydrates our skin and flushes toxins out of our inner organs. It also decreases hunger and promotes weight loss. As adequate water intake replenishes body cells, it also alleviates minor ailments like headaches and can help prevent cramps and strains when exercising. Drinking the appropriate amount of water will keep you feeling healthy and strong so you can spend your days doing things you love!

The challenge this week is to drink half of your weight in ounces every day this week (and hopefully every day from now on).

If you want to watch a life changing video about water — google "dr Emoto water project"

Goals for this week

Health and Fitness

Love and Relationship

Career and Finance

Philanthropy and Giving Back

Shopping list

Hint:
Take a look at your one-year and three-month goals. How can you get closer to achieving them?

Gratitude

Personal
_____

Love & Relationships
_____

Professional
_____

Life
_____

#1 Priority to get me one step closer to achieving my main goal is:
_____

I am going to focus and improve on:
_____

Today is the first day of the rest of my beautiful life, what am I going to do to make a difference?
_____

Daily Reflection

Food Journal

Breakfast
Snack
Lunch
Snack
Dinner
Other

Exercise

RATE YOUR DAY

PERSONAL   LOVE   WORK   OVERALL

Your body is a blank canvas; choose wisely what you put into in.

Monday

Daily To Do

- [ ] Wake up & smile
- [ ] Walk/Run
- [ ] Gratitude
- [ ] Read
- [ ] Meditate
- [ ] Make Bed
- [ ] Donate
- [ ] Exercise
- [ ] Stretch
- [ ] Learn
- [ ] Thank you
- [ ] Day Prep
- [ ] Journal
- [ ] Visualize
- [ ] Water
- [ ] Water
- [ ] Water
- [ ] Go to sleep Happy!

Daily Calendar

5:00
6:00
7:00
8:00
9:00
10:00
11:00
12:00
1:00
2:00
3:00
4:00
5:00
6:00
7:00
8:00
9:00

Daily Focus

People to Contact

To Do Today

Gratitude

Personal

_____

Love & Relationships

_____

Professional

_____

Life

_____

#1 Priority to get me one step closer to achieving my main goal is:

_____

I am going to focus and improve on:

_____

Today is the first day of the rest of my beautiful life, what am I going to do to make a difference?

_____

Daily Reflection

_____
_____
_____
_____
_____
_____
_____
_____
_____
_____

Food Journal

Breakfast

Snack

Lunch

Snack

Dinner

Other

Exercise

RATE YOUR DAY

PERSONAL   LOVE   WORK   OVERALL

Good nutrition creates health in all areas of our existence. – T. Collin Campbell

Daily To Do

- [ ] Wake up & smile
- [ ] Walk/Run
- [ ] Gratitude
- [ ] Read
- [ ] Meditate
- [ ] Make Bed
- [ ] Donate
- [ ] Exercise
- [ ] Stretch
- [ ] Learn
- [ ] Thank you
- [ ] Day Prep
- [ ] Journal
- [ ] Visualize
- [ ] Water
- [ ] Water
- [ ] Water
- [ ] Go to sleep Happy!

Daily Calendar

5:00
6:00
7:00
8:00
9:00
10:00
11:00
12:00
1:00
2:00
3:00
4:00
5:00
6:00
7:00
8:00
9:00

Daily Focus

People to Contact

To Do Today

Gratitude

Personal
_____

Love & Relationships
_____

Professional
_____

Life
_____

#1 Priority to get me one step closer to achieving my main goal is:
_____

I am going to focus and improve on:
_____

Today is the first day of the rest of my beautiful life, what am I going to do to make a difference?
_____

Daily Reflection

Food Journal

Breakfast
Snack
Lunch
Snack
Dinner
Other

Exercise

RATE YOUR DAY

PERSONAL   LOVE   WORK   OVERALL

Wednesday

Daily To Do

- [ ] Wake up & smile
- [ ] Walk/Run
- [ ] Gratitude
- [ ] Read
- [ ] Meditate
- [ ] Make Bed
- [ ] Donate
- [ ] Exercise
- [ ] Stretch
- [ ] Learn
- [ ] Thank you
- [ ] Day Prep
- [ ] Journal
- [ ] Visualize
- [ ] Water
- [ ] Water
- [ ] Water
- [ ] Go to sleep Happy!

Daily Calendar

5:00

6:00

7:00

8:00

9:00

10:00

11:00

12:00

1:00

2:00

3:00

4:00

5:00

6:00

7:00

8:00

9:00

Daily Focus

People to Contact

To Do Today

Gratitude

Personal

_____

Love & Relationships

_____

Professional

_____

Life

_____

#1 Priority to get me one step closer to achieving my main goal is:

_____

I am going to focus and improve on:

_____

Today is the first day of the rest of my beautiful life, what am I going to do to make a difference?

_____

_____

Daily Reflection

Food Journal

Breakfast
Snack
Lunch
Snack
Dinner
Other

Exercise

RATE YOUR DAY

PERSONAL   LOVE   WORK   OVERALL

Let your food be thy medicine and medicine be thy food. – Hippocrates

Daily To Do

- [ ] Wake up & smile
- [ ] Walk/Run
- [ ] Gratitude
- [ ] Read
- [ ] Meditate
- [ ] Make Bed
- [ ] Donate
- [ ] Exercise
- [ ] Stretch
- [ ] Learn
- [ ] Thank you
- [ ] Day Prep
- [ ] Journal
- [ ] Visualize
- [ ] Water
- [ ] Water
- [ ] Water
- [ ] Go to sleep Happy!

Daily Calendar

5:00

6:00

7:00

8:00

9:00

10:00

11:00

12:00

1:00

2:00

3:00

4:00

5:00

6:00

7:00

8:00

9:00

Daily Focus

People to Contact

To Do Today

Gratitude

Personal

_____

Love & Relationships

_____

Professional

_____

Life

_____

#1 Priority to get me one step closer to achieving my main goal is:

_____

I am going to focus and improve on:

_____

Today is the first day of the rest of my beautiful life, what am I going to do to make a difference?

_____

Today is YOUR day
and just by waking up
it is already amazing!

Daily Reflection

Food Journal

Breakfast

Snack

Lunch

Snack

Dinner

Other

Exercise

RATE YOUR DAY

PERSONAL   LOVE   WORK   OVERALL

Health is not about the weight you lose but the life you gain! - Dr Josh Axe

Friday

Daily To Do

- [ ] Wake up & smile
- [ ] Walk/Run
- [ ] Gratitude
- [ ] Read
- [ ] Meditate
- [ ] Make Bed
- [ ] Donate
- [ ] Exercise
- [ ] Stretch
- [ ] Learn
- [ ] Thank you
- [ ] Day Prep
- [ ] Journal
- [ ] Visualize
- [ ] Water
- [ ] Water
- [ ] Water
- [ ] Go to sleep Happy!

Daily Calendar

5:00
6:00
7:00
8:00
9:00
10:00
11:00
12:00
1:00
2:00
3:00
4:00
5:00
6:00
7:00
8:00
9:00

Daily Focus

People to Contact

To Do Today

Gratitude

Personal

Love & Relationships

Professional

Life

#1 Priority to get me one step closer to achieving my main goal is:

I am going to focus and improve on:

Today is the first day of the rest of my beautiful life, what am I going to do to make a difference?

Today is YOUR day and just by waking up it is already amazing!

Daily Reflection

Food Journal

Breakfast

Snack

Lunch

Snack

Dinner

Other

Exercise

RATE YOUR DAY

PERSONAL   LOVE   WORK   OVERALL

You can't control everything in your life, but you
CAN control what you put into your body.

Saturday

Daily To Do

- [ ] Wake up & smile
- [ ] Walk/Run
- [ ] Gratitude
- [ ] Read
- [ ] Meditate
- [ ] Make Bed
- [ ] Donate
- [ ] Exercise
- [ ] Stretch
- [ ] Learn
- [ ] Thank you
- [ ] Day Prep
- [ ] Journal
- [ ] Visualize
- [ ] Water
- [ ] Water
- [ ] Water
- [ ] Go to sleep Happy!

Daily Calendar

5:00
6:00
7:00
8:00
9:00
10:00
11:00
12:00
1:00
2:00
3:00
4:00
5:00
6:00
7:00
8:00
9:00

Daily Focus

People to Contact

To Do Today

Gratitude

Personal
_____

Love & Relationships
_____

Professional
_____

Life
_____

#1 Priority to get me one step closer to achieving my main goal is:
_____

I am going to focus and improve on:
_____

Today is the first day of the rest of my beautiful life, what am I going to do to make a difference?
_____

Today is YOUR day
and just by waking up
it is already amazing!

Daily Reflection

Food Journal

Breakfast
Snack
Lunch
Snack
Dinner
Other

Exercise

RATE YOUR DAY

PERSONAL   LOVE   WORK   OVERALL

A healthy outside starts from the INSIDE. – Robert Urich

Daily To Do

- [ ] Wake up & smile
- [ ] Walk/Run
- [ ] Gratitude
- [ ] Read
- [ ] Meditate
- [ ] Make Bed
- [ ] Donate
- [ ] Exercise
- [ ] Stretch
- [ ] Learn
- [ ] Thank you
- [ ] Day Prep
- [ ] Journal
- [ ] Visualize
- [ ] Water
- [ ] Water
- [ ] Water
- [ ] Go to sleep Happy!

Daily Calendar

5:00
6:00
7:00
8:00
9:00
10:00
11:00
12:00
1:00
2:00
3:00
4:00
5:00
6:00
7:00
8:00
9:00

Daily Focus

People to Contact

To Do Today

Sunday

Today is your day to relax, regroup, reflect and prepare for the next amazing week! What do you feel went really well this past week? List at least 5 accomplishments.

_____

_____

What would you like to improve on for this upcoming week?

_____

_____

What is ONE step that you will take this week to get closer to your dream?

_____

_____

Is there someone that could use your help this week? How can you make a difference?

_____

Weekly Challenge

The challenge this week is to prepare a healthy vegetarian meal for family or friends. Really put some time and effort into creating a beautiful meal using the super foods to fuel our mind, body and soul—then share it with those you love.

Have an amazing Sunday!

Goals for this week

Health and Fitness

Love and Relationship

Career and Finance

Philanthropy and Giving Back

Shopping list

Hint:
Take a look at your one-year and three-month goals. How can you get closer to achieving them?

Love

Love … It's the reason for our existence.

If you are following the steps in the book, you are reading page 20 every morning, and I'm not sure if you have counted or not, but the word 'love' is on that page six times!

There is a reason for that. The more you read it and see it, the more it is on your mind—and as we learned from the Mindset focus, whatever is constantly on your mind you will bring into your world … and who doesn't want more love?

Love is everything. It is getting pleasure from your job or career; sharing a life with someone and starting a family; being able to appreciate the sun shining on your face, or the birds singing outside your window early on a Sunday morning.

Love is waking up excited for life; it's working out and spoiling your body with nutritious foods or following your dreams and helping others achieve theirs.

Love is what makes life worth living—but just like anything else in the world you have to feel it, believe it and give it; in order to receive it.

There have been many studies done about love and some of the benefits might surprise you. In the study, ***Scientific Benefits Of Love: The Positive Effects Of Being In A Happy Relationship***, it talks about how love can help you to live longer, increase your immune system and keep you looking and feeling your best. Love makes absolutely everything better. about the different benefits of love such as make you live longer, help increase your immune system, help you look younger, keep you slim, improve your wellbeing and self-confidence *and* it just feels amazing. Love makes absolutely everything better!

This month, try to live every day like it is your last. It may sound cliché, but give it some meaningful thought and energy; it is cliché for a reason.

Imagine if you only had today left on this earth. Seriously, just take a moment and think about that. What would be important to you? What would you want to do with your very last day?

I can almost guarantee you that you wouldn't be fighting with your spouse about taking out the garbage or leaving dirty clothes on the floor or any other minor irritation. You probably wouldn't be looking in the mirror, pinching your love handles, imagining yourself with bigger pectoral muscles or wishing your nose was smaller.

Would you be telling your kids to go away so you could read your texts or scroll through the web? Or would you be wrapped in the arms of someone you love, or playing and laughing with your kids?

Or would you be phoning your friends and family to tell them how much you love and care for them and expressing gratitude for all the memories you made together. Maybe you would be out in nature taking deep breaths and appreciating every last second … Well why wait until you're dying? Share all that love today and when you wake up tomorrow, you can do it all over again!

Books
The 5 Love Languages – Gary Chapman
The Mastery of Love – Don Miguel Ruiz

YouTube
Manifest Your Partner, Lover, improve your Relationship | Guided Meditation

Affirmation
"I am Love."

Gratitude

Personal

_____

Love & Relationships

_____

Professional

_____

Life

_____

#1 Priority to get me one step closer to achieving my main goal is:

_____

I am going to focus and improve on:

_____

Today is the first day of the rest of my beautiful life, what am I going to do to make a difference?

_____

Today is YOUR day and just by waking up it is already amazing!

Daily Reflection

Food Journal

Breakfast

Snack

Lunch

Snack

Dinner

Other

Exercise

RATE YOUR DAY

PERSONAL   LOVE   WORK   OVERALL

Love is the most powerful force on Earth. – Dallin H. Oaks

Daily To Do

- [ ] Wake up & smile
- [ ] Walk/Run
- [ ] Gratitude
- [ ] Read
- [ ] Meditate
- [ ] Make Bed
- [ ] Donate
- [ ] Exercise
- [ ] Stretch
- [ ] Learn
- [ ] Thank you
- [ ] Day Prep
- [ ] Journal
- [ ] Visualize
- [ ] Water
- [ ] Water
- [ ] Water
- [ ] Go to sleep Happy!

Daily Calendar

5:00
6:00
7:00
8:00
9:00
10:00
11:00
12:00
1:00
2:00
3:00
4:00
5:00
6:00
7:00
8:00
9:00

Daily Focus

People to Contact

To Do Today

Gratitude

Personal

_____

Love & Relationships

_____

Professional

_____

Life

_____

#1 Priority to get me one step closer to achieving my main goal is:

_____

I am going to focus and improve on:

_____

Today is the first day of the rest of my beautiful life, what am I going to do to make a difference?

_____

Daily Reflection

Food Journal

Breakfast
Snack
Lunch
Snack
Dinner
Other

Exercise

RATE YOUR DAY

PERSONAL   LOVE   WORK   OVERALL

Piglet: "How do you spell love?" Pooh: "You don't spell love, you feel it."

Daily To Do

- [ ] Wake up & smile
- [ ] Walk/Run
- [ ] Gratitude
- [ ] Read
- [ ] Meditate
- [ ] Make Bed
- [ ] Donate
- [ ] Exercise
- [ ] Stretch
- [ ] Learn
- [ ] Thank you
- [ ] Day Prep
- [ ] Journal
- [ ] Visualize
- [ ] Water
- [ ] Water
- [ ] Water
- [ ] Go to sleep Happy!

Daily Calendar

5:00

6:00

7:00

8:00

9:00

10:00

11:00

12:00

1:00

2:00

3:00

4:00

5:00

6:00

7:00

8:00

9:00

Daily Focus

People to Contact

To Do Today

Gratitude

Personal
_____

Love & Relationships
_____

Professional
_____

Life
_____

#1 Priority to get me one step closer to achieving my main goal is:
_____

I am going to focus and improve on:
_____

Today is the first day of the rest of my beautiful life, what am I going to do to make a difference?
_____

Daily Reflection
_____
_____
_____
_____
_____
_____
_____
_____
_____
_____
_____
_____
_____

Food Journal

Breakfast
Snack
Lunch
Snack
Dinner
Other

Exercise

RATE YOUR DAY

PERSONAL   LOVE   WORK   OVERALL

Wednesday

Daily To Do

- [ ] Wake up & smile
- [ ] Walk/Run
- [ ] Gratitude
- [ ] Read
- [ ] Meditate
- [ ] Make Bed
- [ ] Donate
- [ ] Exercise
- [ ] Stretch
- [ ] Learn
- [ ] Thank you
- [ ] Day Prep
- [ ] Journal
- [ ] Visualize
- [ ] Water
- [ ] Water
- [ ] Water
- [ ] Go to sleep Happy!

Daily Calendar

5:00

6:00

7:00

8:00

9:00

10:00

11:00

12:00

1:00

2:00

3:00

4:00

5:00

6:00

7:00

8:00

9:00

Daily Focus

People to Contact

To Do Today

Gratitude

Personal
_____

Love & Relationships
_____

Professional
_____

Life
_____

#1 Priority to get me one step closer to achieving my main goal is:
_____

I am going to focus and improve on:
_____

Today is the first day of the rest of my beautiful life, what am I going to do to make a difference?
_____
_____

Today is YOUR day and just by waking up it is already amazing!

Daily Reflection
_____
_____
_____
_____
_____
_____
_____
_____
_____
_____
_____

Food Journal

Breakfast
Snack
Lunch
Snack
Dinner
Other

Exercise

RATE YOUR DAY

PERSONAL   LOVE   WORK   OVERALL

Daily To Do

- [ ] Wake up & smile
- [ ] Walk/Run
- [ ] Gratitude
- [ ] Read
- [ ] Meditate
- [ ] Make Bed
- [ ] Donate
- [ ] Exercise
- [ ] Stretch
- [ ] Learn
- [ ] Thank you
- [ ] Day Prep
- [ ] Journal
- [ ] Visualize
- [ ] Water
- [ ] Water
- [ ] Water
- [ ] Go to sleep Happy!

Daily Calendar

5:00

6:00

7:00

8:00

9:00

10:00

11:00

12:00

1:00

2:00

3:00

4:00

5:00

6:00

7:00

8:00

9:00

Daily Focus

People to Contact

To Do Today

Gratitude

Personal
_____

Love & Relationships
_____

Professional
_____

Life
_____

#1 Priority to get me one step closer to achieving my main goal is:
_____

I am going to focus and improve on:
_____

Today is the first day of the rest of my beautiful life, what am I going to do to make a difference?
_____

Daily Reflection

Food Journal

Breakfast
Snack
Lunch
Snack
Dinner
Other

Exercise

RATE YOUR DAY

PERSONAL   LOVE   WORK   OVERALL

Friday

Daily To Do

- ☐ Wake up & smile
- ☐ Walk/Run
- ☐ Gratitude
- ☐ Read
- ☐ Meditate
- ☐ Make Bed
- ☐ Donate
- ☐ Exercise
- ☐ Stretch
- ☐ Learn
- ☐ Thank you
- ☐ Day Prep
- ☐ Journal
- ☐ Visualize
- ☐ Water
- ☐ Water
- ☐ Water
- ☐ Go to sleep Happy!

Daily Calendar

5:00
6:00
7:00
8:00
9:00
10:00
11:00
12:00
1:00
2:00
3:00
4:00
5:00
6:00
7:00
8:00
9:00

Daily Focus

People to Contact

To Do Today

Gratitude

Personal
_____

Love & Relationships
_____

Professional
_____

Life
_____

#1 Priority to get me one step closer to achieving my main goal is:
_____

I am going to focus and improve on:
_____

Today is the first day of the rest of my beautiful life, what am I going to do to make a difference?
_____

Daily Reflection

Food Journal

Breakfast
Snack
Lunch
Snack
Dinner
Other

Exercise

RATE YOUR DAY

PERSONAL   LOVE   WORK   OVERALL

Love is the master key which opens the gates of happiness. – Oliver Wendall Holmes

Saturday

Daily To Do

- [ ] Wake up & smile
- [ ] Walk/Run
- [ ] Gratitude
- [ ] Read
- [ ] Meditate
- [ ] Make Bed
- [ ] Donate
- [ ] Exercise
- [ ] Stretch
- [ ] Learn
- [ ] Thank you
- [ ] Day Prep
- [ ] Journal
- [ ] Visualize
- [ ] Water
- [ ] Water
- [ ] Water
- [ ] Go to sleep Happy!

Daily Calendar

5:00
6:00
7:00
8:00
9:00
10:00
11:00
12:00
1:00
2:00
3:00
4:00
5:00
6:00
7:00
8:00
9:00

Daily Focus

People to Contact

To Do Today

Gratitude

Personal
_____

Love & Relationships
_____

Professional
_____

Life
_____

#1 Priority to get me one step closer to achieving my main goal is:
_____

I am going to focus and improve on:
_____

Today is the first day of the rest of my beautiful life, what am I going to do to make a difference?
_____

Daily Reflection
_____
_____
_____
_____
_____
_____
_____
_____
_____
_____
_____

Food Journal

Breakfast
Snack
Lunch
Snack
Dinner
Other

Exercise

RATE YOUR DAY

PERSONAL   LOVE   WORK   OVERALL

Daily To Do

- [ ] Wake up & smile
- [ ] Walk/Run
- [ ] Gratitude
- [ ] Read
- [ ] Meditate
- [ ] Make Bed
- [ ] Donate
- [ ] Exercise
- [ ] Stretch
- [ ] Learn
- [ ] Thank you
- [ ] Day Prep
- [ ] Journal
- [ ] Visualize
- [ ] Water
- [ ] Water
- [ ] Water
- [ ] Go to sleep Happy!

Daily Calendar

5:00

6:00

7:00

8:00

9:00

10:00

11:00

12:00

1:00

2:00

3:00

4:00

5:00

6:00

7:00

8:00

9:00

Daily Focus

People to Contact

To Do Today

Sunday

Today is your day to relax, regroup, reflect and prepare for the next amazing week! What do you feel went really well this past week? List at least 5 accomplishments.

_____

_____

What would you like to improve on for this upcoming week?

_____

_____

What is ONE step that you will take this week to get closer to your dream?

_____

_____

Is there someone that could use your help this week? How can you make a difference?

_____

Weekly Challenge

The challenge this week is to write out 50 things that you love about your spouse. It may seem like a big number, but I bet there are far more than 50 things you could write (so feel free to keep going!). You can write about the things they do; funny memories you have together; their physical appearance; the way they parent your children; how they treat you, hold you, kiss you; all the ways that meeting them has changed your life; their character and drive ... there are so many things that make the people close to us special, write them out and get more of those good thoughts flowing. When you're done, leave the list out somewhere for them to see, give it to them or maybe even read it to them!

If you haven't met your perfect partner yet, you still can challenge yourself in this way! Your list will be what you will be grateful for—and love about your future perfect partner—once he or she is in your life.

Write out all the qualities you want in your future spouse. Getting clear on exactly what you are looking for will draw them into your life fast!

Goals for this week

Health and Fitness

Love and Relationship

Career and Finance

Philanthropy and Giving Back

Shopping list

Hint:
Take a look at your one-year and three-month goals. How can you get closer to achieving them?

Gratitude

Personal
_____

Love & Relationships
_____

Professional
_____

Life
_____

#1 Priority to get me one step closer to achieving my main goal is:
_____

I am going to focus and improve on:
_____

Today is the first day of the rest of my beautiful life, what am I going to do to make a difference?
_____

Daily Reflection

_____
_____
_____
_____
_____
_____
_____
_____
_____
_____

Food Journal

Breakfast
Snack
Lunch
Snack
Dinner
Other

Exercise

RATE YOUR DAY

PERSONAL   LOVE   WORK   OVERALL

Daily To Do

- ☐ Wake up & smile
- ☐ Walk/Run
- ☐ Gratitude
- ☐ Read
- ☐ Meditate
- ☐ Make Bed
- ☐ Donate
- ☐ Exercise
- ☐ Stretch
- ☐ Learn
- ☐ Thank you
- ☐ Day Prep
- ☐ Journal
- ☐ Visualize
- ☐ Water
- ☐ Water
- ☐ Water
- ☐ Go to sleep Happy!

Daily Calendar

5:00

6:00

7:00

8:00

9:00

10:00

11:00

12:00

1:00

2:00

3:00

4:00

5:00

6:00

7:00

8:00

9:00

Daily Focus

People to Contact

To Do Today

Gratitude

Personal
_____

Love & Relationships
_____

Professional
_____

Life
_____

#1 Priority to get me one step closer to achieving my main goal is:
_____

I am going to focus and improve on:
_____

Today is the first day of the rest of my beautiful life, what am I going to do to make a difference?
_____

Today is YOUR day and just by waking up it is already amazing!

Daily Reflection

Food Journal

Breakfast
Snack
Lunch
Snack
Dinner
Other

Exercise

RATE YOUR DAY

PERSONAL   LOVE   WORK   OVERALL

Let us always meet each other with a smile, for the smile is the beginning of love. – Mother Teresa

Tuesday

Daily To Do

- ☐ Wake up & smile
- ☐ Walk/Run
- ☐ Gratitude
- ☐ Read
- ☐ Meditate
- ☐ Make Bed
- ☐ Donate
- ☐ Exercise
- ☐ Stretch
- ☐ Learn
- ☐ Thank you
- ☐ Day Prep
- ☐ Journal
- ☐ Visualize
- ☐ Water
- ☐ Water
- ☐ Water
- ☐ Go to sleep Happy!

Daily Calendar

5:00
6:00
7:00
8:00
9:00
10:00
11:00
12:00
1:00
2:00
3:00
4:00
5:00
6:00
7:00
8:00
9:00

Daily Focus

People to Contact

To Do Today

Gratitude

Personal
_____

Love & Relationships
_____

Professional
_____

Life
_____

#1 Priority to get me one step closer to achieving my main goal is:
_____

I am going to focus and improve on:
_____

Today is the first day of the rest of my beautiful life, what am I going to do to make a difference?
_____

Daily Reflection

Food Journal

Breakfast
Snack
Lunch
Snack
Dinner
Other

Exercise

RATE YOUR DAY

PERSONAL   LOVE   WORK   OVERALL

Daily To Do

- [ ] Wake up & smile
- [ ] Walk/Run
- [ ] Gratitude
- [ ] Read
- [ ] Meditate
- [ ] Make Bed
- [ ] Donate
- [ ] Exercise
- [ ] Stretch
- [ ] Learn
- [ ] Thank you
- [ ] Day Prep
- [ ] Journal
- [ ] Visualize
- [ ] Water
- [ ] Water
- [ ] Water
- [ ] Go to sleep Happy!

Daily Calendar

5:00

6:00

7:00

8:00

9:00

10:00

11:00

12:00

1:00

2:00

3:00

4:00

5:00

6:00

7:00

8:00

9:00

Daily Focus

People to Contact

To Do Today

Gratitude

Personal
_____

Love & Relationships
_____

Professional
_____

Life
_____

#1 Priority to get me one step closer to achieving my main goal is:
_____

I am going to focus and improve on:
_____

Today is the first day of the rest of my beautiful life, what am I going to do to make a difference?
_____

Today is YOUR day
and just by waking up
it is already amazing!

Daily Reflection

_____
_____
_____
_____
_____
_____
_____
_____
_____
_____
_____

Food Journal

Breakfast
Snack
Lunch
Snack
Dinner
Other

Exercise

RATE YOUR DAY

PERSONAL   LOVE   WORK   OVERALL

A heart filled with love is always young.

Daily To Do

- ☐ Wake up & smile
- ☐ Walk/Run
- ☐ Gratitude
- ☐ Read
- ☐ Meditate
- ☐ Make Bed
- ☐ Donate
- ☐ Exercise
- ☐ Stretch
- ☐ Learn
- ☐ Thank you
- ☐ Day Prep
- ☐ Journal
- ☐ Visualize
- ☐ Water
- ☐ Water
- ☐ Water
- ☐ Go to sleep Happy!

Daily Calendar

5:00

6:00

7:00

8:00

9:00

10:00

11:00

12:00

1:00

2:00

3:00

4:00

5:00

6:00

7:00

8:00

9:00

Daily Focus

People to Contact

To Do Today

Gratitude

Personal
_____

Love & Relationships
_____

Professional
_____

Life
_____

#1 Priority to get me one step closer to achieving my main goal is:
_____

I am going to focus and improve on:
_____

Today is the first day of the rest of my beautiful life, what am I going to do to make a difference?
_____

Today is YOUR day
and just by waking up
it is already amazing!

Daily Reflection
_____
_____
_____
_____
_____
_____
_____
_____
_____
_____

Food Journal

Breakfast
Snack
Lunch
Snack
Dinner
Other

Exercise

RATE YOUR DAY

PERSONAL   LOVE   WORK   OVERALL

If you wish to be loved, then love! – Seneca

Friday

Daily To Do

- [ ] Wake up & smile
- [ ] Walk/Run
- [ ] Gratitude
- [ ] Read
- [ ] Meditate
- [ ] Make Bed
- [ ] Donate
- [ ] Exercise
- [ ] Stretch
- [ ] Learn
- [ ] Thank you
- [ ] Day Prep
- [ ] Journal
- [ ] Visualize
- [ ] Water
- [ ] Water
- [ ] Water
- [ ] Go to sleep Happy!

Daily Calendar

5:00
6:00
7:00
8:00
9:00
10:00
11:00
12:00
1:00
2:00
3:00
4:00
5:00
6:00
7:00
8:00
9:00

Daily Focus

People to Contact

To Do Today

Gratitude

Personal
_____

Love & Relationships
_____

Professional
_____

Life
_____

#1 Priority to get me one step closer to achieving my main goal is:
_____

I am going to focus and improve on:
_____

Today is the first day of the rest of my beautiful life, what am I going to do to make a difference?
_____

Daily Reflection

Food Journal

Breakfast
Snack
Lunch
Snack
Dinner
Other

Exercise

RATE YOUR DAY

PERSONAL   LOVE   WORK   OVERALL

Daily To Do

- [ ] Wake up & smile
- [ ] Walk/Run
- [ ] Gratitude
- [ ] Read
- [ ] Meditate
- [ ] Make Bed
- [ ] Donate
- [ ] Exercise
- [ ] Stretch
- [ ] Learn
- [ ] Thank you
- [ ] Day Prep
- [ ] Journal
- [ ] Visualize
- [ ] Water
- [ ] Water
- [ ] Water
- [ ] Go to sleep Happy!

Daily Calendar

5:00

6:00

7:00

8:00

9:00

10:00

11:00

12:00

1:00

2:00

3:00

4:00

5:00

6:00

7:00

8:00

9:00

Daily Focus

People to Contact

To Do Today

Gratitude

Personal
_____

Love & Relationships
_____

Professional
_____

Life
_____

#1 Priority to get me one step closer to achieving my main goal is:
_____

I am going to focus and improve on:
_____

Today is the first day of the rest of my beautiful life, what am I going to do to make a difference?
_____

Daily Reflection

_____
_____
_____
_____
_____
_____
_____
_____
_____
_____
_____

Food Journal

Breakfast
Snack
Lunch
Snack
Dinner
Other

Exercise

RATE YOUR DAY

PERSONAL   LOVE   WORK   OVERALL

Love makes the world go round.

Sunday

Daily To Do

- ☐ Wake up & smile
- ☐ Walk/Run
- ☐ Gratitude
- ☐ Read
- ☐ Meditate
- ☐ Make Bed
- ☐ Donate
- ☐ Exercise
- ☐ Stretch
- ☐ Learn
- ☐ Thank you
- ☐ Day Prep
- ☐ Journal
- ☐ Visualize
- ☐ Water
- ☐ Water
- ☐ Water
- ☐ Go to sleep Happy!

Daily Calendar

5:00
6:00
7:00
8:00
9:00
10:00
11:00
12:00
1:00
2:00
3:00
4:00
5:00
6:00
7:00
8:00
9:00

Daily Focus

People to Contact

To Do Today

Sunday

Today is your day to relax, regroup, reflect and prepare for the next amazing week! What do you feel went really well this past week? List at least 5 accomplishments.

_____

_____

What would you like to improve on for this upcoming week?

_____

_____

What is ONE step that you will take this week to get closer to your dream?

_____

_____

Is there someone that could use your help this week? How can you make a difference?

_____

Weekly Challenge

The challenge this week is to plan a date night with your partner. Really take some time to think about your spouse and what they love to do. Maybe he or she loves hiking and taking a picnic along. Maybe they prefer, bowling, going to a hockey game, a home-cooked meal, a massage, a movie or just finally having a night alone! Make sure you plan it on a day that you both have time to get ready for each other. Get dressed up, get excited, think about all the things that you want to say and do with each other.

Not in a relationship? Sweet—you have the same challenge! You could take a friend, or you could just take yourself out. You never know, maybe your dream person will be there waiting! Just go. And have a wonderful time.

Goals for this week

Health and Fitness

Love and Relationship

Career and Finance

Philanthropy and Giving Back

Hint:
Take a look at your one-year and three-month goals. How can you get closer to achieving them?

Shopping list

Philanthropy

I love the idea of giving back and I love the feeling of giving back!

I am a firm believer in karma—I believe that whatever a person puts out into the world will be returned back to them (and usually tenfold). If you are sending true love and kindness out in to the world, you will receive all of the love and kindness you can imagine. If you are volunteering your time and helping other people, you will find that you have more than enough time for all the other important things in your life. If you believe that you have more than enough money to spare and share and give financial support to charities that really speak to your soul, then give, and that money will come back to you tenfold. The key is to tithe, make offerings or volunteer with an open heart! Do charitable works for the joy of bringing love into someone else's life, not just to get something in return.

This was one thing that really stood out when researching and studying all the successful people whose works spoke to me—they either started their own charity or foundation or they support an existing one they believe in. We rarely hear about all the amazing things that happen behind the scenes in the lives of these people because they don't do it for recognition; they do it because they can and because it feels good to help other people, animals and our planet.

We are all here on Earth together; why not try to make it the best possible experience you can for your fellow inhabitants?

A lot of people have good intentions and say such things as, "when I am rich I will donate," or "when I make partner I am going to have more free time on my hands and I will coach my kid's softball team then."

Don't put charitable works off. Now is the time to do them! Now is going to make the difference in your life. Donating money to a good cause or volunteering will release feelings you've never felt before. It will bring positivity and good things into your life more quickly than you can ever imagine and put some big 'money' in your Karma bank—and this is the greatest bank in the world, it cannot fail!

If you are presently short on money, then just donate what you can with all your heart. The amount doesn't really matter; it is the love and thought you send with it that counts. If you have just fifty cents to give then do it, but do it knowing that it is still going to make a difference. You are being selfless and helping someone or something else.

If you have a closet full of clothing that you have not worn in years, go through it! Not only will de-cluttering actually improve your frame of mind, but donating your clothes to charity will improve someone else's life too. They will have new-to-them clothing to wear that will make them feel beautiful or handsome.

With all the material things we have in our lives, sometimes we forget how truly blessed we are. Please take a look around your home; are there things you don't use? Things you keep around just in case you need them when you probably won't use them at all? These things could actually be out in the world being used daily by someone in need. So give them away!

The book recommendation could be a game changer for you. I hope you enjoy it as much as I did.

Book Recommendation
The Life Changing Magic of Tidying Up – Marie Kondo
Think and Grow Rich – Napoleon Hill

YouTube/Internet
How to become a money magnet – YouAreCreators

Affirmation
"I always have enough money to spare and share"

Gratitude

Personal

_____

Love & Relationships

_____

Professional

_____

Life

_____

#1 Priority to get me one step closer to achieving my main goal is:

_____

I am going to focus and improve on:

_____

Today is the first day of the rest of my beautiful life, what am I going to do to make a difference?

_____

Daily Reflection

Food Journal

Breakfast
Snack
Lunch
Snack
Dinner
Other

Exercise

RATE YOUR DAY

PERSONAL   LOVE   WORK   OVERALL

Be the person who creates positive ripple effects. - Camilla Kragius

Daily To Do

☐ Wake up & smile

☐ Walk/Run

☐ Gratitude

☐ Read

☐ Meditate

☐ Make Bed

☐ Donate

☐ Exercise

☐ Stretch

☐ Learn

☐ Thank you

☐ Day Prep

☐ Journal

☐ Visualize

☐ Water

☐ Water

☐ Water

☐ Go to sleep Happy!

Daily Calendar

5:00

6:00

7:00

8:00

9:00

10:00

11:00

12:00

1:00

2:00

3:00

4:00

5:00

6:00

7:00

8:00

9:00

Daily Focus

People to Contact

To Do Today

Gratitude

Personal
_____

Love & Relationships
_____

Professional
_____

Life
_____

#1 Priority to get me one step closer to achieving my main goal is:
_____

I am going to focus and improve on:
_____

Today is the first day of the rest of my beautiful life, what am I going to do to make a difference?
_____

Daily Reflection
_____
_____
_____
_____
_____
_____
_____
_____
_____
_____
_____

Food Journal

Breakfast _____
Snack _____
Lunch _____
Snack _____
Dinner _____
Other _____

Exercise
_____
_____

RATE YOUR DAY

PERSONAL   LOVE   WORK   OVERALL

No act of kindness, no matter how small, is ever wasted. - Aesop

Daily To Do

- [ ] Wake up & smile
- [ ] Walk/Run
- [ ] Gratitude
- [ ] Read
- [ ] Meditate
- [ ] Make Bed
- [ ] Donate
- [ ] Exercise
- [ ] Stretch
- [ ] Learn
- [ ] Thank you
- [ ] Day Prep
- [ ] Journal
- [ ] Visualize
- [ ] Water
- [ ] Water
- [ ] Water
- [ ] Go to sleep Happy!

Daily Calendar

5:00
6:00
7:00
8:00
9:00
10:00
11:00
12:00
1:00
2:00
3:00
4:00
5:00
6:00
7:00
8:00
9:00

Daily Focus

People to Contact

To Do Today

Gratitude

Personal
_____

Love & Relationships
_____

Professional
_____

Life
_____

#1 Priority to get me one step closer to achieving my main goal is:
_____

I am going to focus and improve on:
_____

Today is the first day of the rest of my beautiful life, what am I going to do to make a difference?
_____

Daily Reflection

Food Journal

Breakfast
Snack
Lunch
Snack
Dinner
Other

Exercise

RATE YOUR DAY

PERSONAL   LOVE   WORK   OVERALL

The best way to find yourself is to get lost in the service of others. - Mahatma Gandi

Daily To Do

- [ ] Wake up & smile
- [ ] Walk/Run
- [ ] Gratitude
- [ ] Read
- [ ] Meditate
- [ ] Make Bed
- [ ] Donate
- [ ] Exercise
- [ ] Stretch
- [ ] Learn
- [ ] Thank you
- [ ] Day Prep
- [ ] Journal
- [ ] Visualize
- [ ] Water
- [ ] Water
- [ ] Water
- [ ] Go to sleep Happy!

Daily Calendar

5:00

6:00

7:00

8:00

9:00

10:00

11:00

12:00

1:00

2:00

3:00

4:00

5:00

6:00

7:00

8:00

9:00

Daily Focus

People to Contact

To Do Today

Gratitude

Personal
_____

Love & Relationships
_____

Professional
_____

Life
_____

#1 Priority to get me one step closer to achieving my main goal is:
_____

I am going to focus and improve on:
_____

Today is the first day of the rest of my beautiful life, what am I going to do to make a difference?
_____

Daily Reflection

_____
_____
_____
_____
_____
_____
_____
_____
_____
_____
_____

Food Journal

Breakfast
Snack
Lunch
Snack
Dinner
Other

Exercise

RATE YOUR DAY

PERSONAL   LOVE   WORK   OVERALL

Thursday

Daily To Do

- [ ] Wake up & smile
- [ ] Walk/Run
- [ ] Gratitude
- [ ] Read
- [ ] Meditate
- [ ] Make Bed
- [ ] Donate
- [ ] Exercise
- [ ] Stretch
- [ ] Learn
- [ ] Thank you
- [ ] Day Prep
- [ ] Journal
- [ ] Visualize
- [ ] Water
- [ ] Water
- [ ] Water
- [ ] Go to sleep Happy!

Daily Calendar

5:00

6:00

7:00

8:00

9:00

10:00

11:00

12:00

1:00

2:00

3:00

4:00

5:00

6:00

7:00

8:00

9:00

Daily Focus

People to Contact

To Do Today

Gratitude

Personal
_____

Love & Relationships
_____

Professional
_____

Life
_____

#1 Priority to get me one step closer to achieving my main goal is:
_____

I am going to focus and improve on:
_____

Today is the first day of the rest of my beautiful life, what am I going to do to make a difference?
_____

Daily Reflection
_____
_____
_____
_____
_____
_____
_____
_____
_____
_____
_____
_____

Food Journal

Breakfast
Snack
Lunch
Snack
Dinner
Other

Exercise

RATE YOUR DAY

PERSONAL   LOVE   WORK   OVERALL

When you learn, teach. When you get, give. - Maya Angelou

Friday

Daily To Do

- [ ] Wake up & smile
- [ ] Walk/Run
- [ ] Gratitude
- [ ] Read
- [ ] Meditate
- [ ] Make Bed
- [ ] Donate
- [ ] Exercise
- [ ] Stretch
- [ ] Learn
- [ ] Thank you
- [ ] Day Prep
- [ ] Journal
- [ ] Visualize
- [ ] Water
- [ ] Water
- [ ] Water
- [ ] Go to sleep Happy!

Daily Calendar

5:00

6:00

7:00

8:00

9:00

10:00

11:00

12:00

1:00

2:00

3:00

4:00

5:00

6:00

7:00

8:00

9:00

Daily Focus

People to Contact

To Do Today

Gratitude

Personal

_____

Love & Relationships

_____

Professional

_____

Life

_____

#1 Priority to get me one step closer to achieving my main goal is:

_____

I am going to focus and improve on:

_____

Today is the first day of the rest of my beautiful life, what am I going to do to make a difference?

_____

Daily Reflection

_____
_____
_____
_____
_____
_____
_____
_____
_____
_____
_____

Food Journal

Breakfast
Snack
Lunch
Snack
Dinner
Other

Exercise

RATE YOUR DAY

PERSONAL   LOVE   WORK   OVERALL

Daily To Do

- [ ] Wake up & smile
- [ ] Walk/Run
- [ ] Gratitude
- [ ] Read
- [ ] Meditate
- [ ] Make Bed
- [ ] Donate
- [ ] Exercise
- [ ] Stretch
- [ ] Learn
- [ ] Thank you
- [ ] Day Prep
- [ ] Journal
- [ ] Visualize
- [ ] Water
- [ ] Water
- [ ] Water
- [ ] Go to sleep Happy!

Daily Calendar

5:00

6:00

7:00

8:00

9:00

10:00

11:00

12:00

1:00

2:00

3:00

4:00

5:00

6:00

7:00

8:00

9:00

Daily Focus

People to Contact

To Do Today

Gratitude

Personal

_____

Love & Relationships

_____

Professional

_____

Life

_____

#1 Priority to get me one step closer to achieving my main goal is:

_____

I am going to focus and improve on:

_____

Today is the first day of the rest of my beautiful life, what am I going to do to make a difference?

_____

Daily Reflection

Food Journal

Breakfast

Snack

Lunch

Snack

Dinner

Other

Exercise

RATE YOUR DAY

PERSONAL   LOVE   WORK   OVERALL

Daily To Do

- [ ] Wake up & smile
- [ ] Walk/Run
- [ ] Gratitude
- [ ] Read
- [ ] Meditate
- [ ] Make Bed
- [ ] Donate
- [ ] Exercise
- [ ] Stretch
- [ ] Learn
- [ ] Thank you
- [ ] Day Prep
- [ ] Journal
- [ ] Visualize
- [ ] Water
- [ ] Water
- [ ] Water
- [ ] Go to sleep Happy!

Daily Calendar

5:00

6:00

7:00

8:00

9:00

10:00

11:00

12:00

1:00

2:00

3:00

4:00

5:00

6:00

7:00

8:00

9:00

Daily Focus

People to Contact

To Do Today

Sunday

Today is your day to relax, regroup, reflect and prepare for the next amazing week! What do you feel went really well this past week? List at least 5 accomplishments.

_____

_____

What would you like to improve on for this upcoming week?

_____

_____

What is ONE step that you will take this week to get closer to your dream?

_____

_____

Is there someone that could use your help this week? How can you make a difference?

_____

Weekly Challenge

The challenge this week is to make a major philanthropy goal.

Perhaps your goal is to host an annual gala that will raise money and awareness for marriage equality. Or maybe you want to save up $25,000.00 in the next 10 years to build a school for a village in Honduras. Perhaps you want to send out 10 Shelter Boxes to countries in need?

These are BIG goals—but big challenges create big achievements and big achievements feel AMAZING!

Goals for this week

Health and Fitness

Love and Relationship

Career and Finance

Philanthropy and Giving Back

Hint:
Take a look at your one-year and three-month goals. How can you get closer to achieving them?

Shopping list

Gratitude

Personal
_____

Love & Relationships
_____

Professional
_____

Life
_____

#1 Priority to get me one step closer to achieving my main goal is:
_____

I am going to focus and improve on:
_____

Today is the first day of the rest of my beautiful life, what am I going to do to make a difference?
_____

Daily Reflection
_____
_____
_____
_____
_____
_____
_____
_____
_____
_____
_____

Food Journal

Breakfast _____
Snack _____
Lunch _____
Snack _____
Dinner _____
Other _____

Exercise
_____
_____

RATE YOUR DAY

PERSONAL   LOVE   WORK   OVERALL

Giving is not just about making a donation; it's about making a difference. - Kathy Calvin

Daily To Do

- ☐ Wake up & smile
- ☐ Walk/Run
- ☐ Gratitude
- ☐ Read
- ☐ Meditate
- ☐ Make Bed
- ☐ Donate
- ☐ Exercise
- ☐ Stretch
- ☐ Learn
- ☐ Thank you
- ☐ Day Prep
- ☐ Journal
- ☐ Visualize
- ☐ Water
- ☐ Water
- ☐ Water
- ☐ Go to sleep Happy!

Daily Calendar

5:00

6:00

7:00

8:00

9:00

10:00

11:00

12:00

1:00

2:00

3:00

4:00

5:00

6:00

7:00

8:00

9:00

Daily Focus

People to Contact

To Do Today

Gratitude

Personal

_____

Love & Relationships

_____

Professional

_____

Life

_____

#1 Priority to get me one step closer to achieving my main goal is:

_____

I am going to focus and improve on:

_____

Today is the first day of the rest of my beautiful life, what am I going to do to make a difference?

_____

Today is YOUR day and just by waking up it is already amazing!

Daily Reflection

Food Journal

Breakfast

Snack

Lunch

Snack

Dinner

Other

Exercise

RATE YOUR DAY

PERSONAL   LOVE   WORK   OVERALL

Life is truly a boomerang. What you give, you get. - Dale Carnegie

Daily To Do

- [ ] Wake up & smile
- [ ] Walk/Run
- [ ] Gratitude
- [ ] Read
- [ ] Meditate
- [ ] Make Bed
- [ ] Donate
- [ ] Exercise
- [ ] Stretch
- [ ] Learn
- [ ] Thank you
- [ ] Day Prep
- [ ] Journal
- [ ] Visualize
- [ ] Water
- [ ] Water
- [ ] Water
- [ ] Go to sleep Happy!

Daily Calendar

5:00
6:00
7:00
8:00
9:00
10:00
11:00
12:00
1:00
2:00
3:00
4:00
5:00
6:00
7:00
8:00
9:00

Daily Focus

People to Contact

To Do Today

Gratitude

Personal
_____

Love & Relationships
_____

Professional
_____

Life
_____

#1 Priority to get me one step closer to achieving my main goal is:
_____

I am going to focus and improve on:
_____

Today is the first day of the rest of my beautiful life, what am I going to do to make a difference?
_____

Daily Reflection

_____
_____
_____
_____
_____
_____
_____
_____
_____
_____
_____
_____

Food Journal

Breakfast
Snack
Lunch
Snack
Dinner
Other

Exercise

RATE YOUR DAY

PERSONAL   LOVE   WORK   OVERALL

Daily To Do

- [ ] Wake up & smile
- [ ] Walk/Run
- [ ] Gratitude
- [ ] Read
- [ ] Meditate
- [ ] Make Bed
- [ ] Donate
- [ ] Exercise
- [ ] Stretch
- [ ] Learn
- [ ] Thank you
- [ ] Day Prep
- [ ] Journal
- [ ] Visualize
- [ ] Water
- [ ] Water
- [ ] Water
- [ ] Go to sleep Happy!

Daily Calendar

5:00

6:00

7:00

8:00

9:00

10:00

11:00

12:00

1:00

2:00

3:00

4:00

5:00

6:00

7:00

8:00

9:00

Daily Focus

People to Contact

To Do Today

Gratitude

Personal
_____

Love & Relationships
_____

Professional
_____

Life
_____

#1 Priority to get me one step closer to achieving my main goal is:
_____

I am going to focus and improve on:
_____

Today is the first day of the rest of my beautiful life, what am I going to do to make a difference?
_____

Daily Reflection

Food Journal

Breakfast
Snack
Lunch
Snack
Dinner
Other

Exercise

RATE YOUR DAY

PERSONAL   LOVE   WORK   OVERALL

Daily To Do

- [ ] Wake up & smile
- [ ] Walk/Run
- [ ] Gratitude
- [ ] Read
- [ ] Meditate
- [ ] Make Bed
- [ ] Donate
- [ ] Exercise
- [ ] Stretch
- [ ] Learn
- [ ] Thank you
- [ ] Day Prep
- [ ] Journal
- [ ] Visualize
- [ ] Water
- [ ] Water
- [ ] Water
- [ ] Go to sleep Happy!

Daily Calendar

5:00

6:00

7:00

8:00

9:00

10:00

11:00

12:00

1:00

2:00

3:00

4:00

5:00

6:00

7:00

8:00

9:00

Daily Focus

People to Contact

To Do Today

Gratitude

Personal

Love & Relationships

Professional

Life

#1 Priority to get me one step closer to achieving my main goal is:

I am going to focus and improve on:

Today is the first day of the rest of my beautiful life, what am I going to do to make a difference?

Today is YOUR day and just by waking up it is already amazing!

Daily Reflection

Food Journal

Breakfast

Snack

Lunch

Snack

Dinner

Other

Exercise

RATE YOUR DAY

PERSONAL   LOVE   WORK   OVERALL

Daily To Do

- [ ] Wake up & smile
- [ ] Walk/Run
- [ ] Gratitude
- [ ] Read
- [ ] Meditate
- [ ] Make Bed
- [ ] Donate
- [ ] Exercise
- [ ] Stretch
- [ ] Learn
- [ ] Thank you
- [ ] Day Prep
- [ ] Journal
- [ ] Visualize
- [ ] Water
- [ ] Water
- [ ] Water
- [ ] Go to sleep Happy!

Daily Calendar

5:00
6:00
7:00
8:00
9:00
10:00
11:00
12:00
1:00
2:00
3:00
4:00
5:00
6:00
7:00
8:00
9:00

Daily Focus

People to Contact

To Do Today

Gratitude

Personal
_____

Love & Relationships
_____

Professional
_____

Life
_____

#1 Priority to get me one step closer to achieving my main goal is:
_____

I am going to focus and improve on:
_____

Today is the first day of the rest of my beautiful life, what am I going to do to make a difference?
_____

Daily Reflection
_____
_____
_____
_____
_____
_____
_____
_____
_____
_____
_____

Food Journal

Breakfast _____
Snack _____
Lunch _____
Snack _____
Dinner _____
Other _____

Exercise
_____
_____

RATE YOUR DAY

PERSONAL   LOVE   WORK   OVERALL

Greatness lies, not in being strong, but in the right using of strength. - Henry Ward Beecher

Daily To Do

- [ ] Wake up & smile
- [ ] Walk/Run
- [ ] Gratitude
- [ ] Read
- [ ] Meditate
- [ ] Make Bed
- [ ] Donate
- [ ] Exercise
- [ ] Stretch
- [ ] Learn
- [ ] Thank you
- [ ] Day Prep
- [ ] Journal
- [ ] Visualize
- [ ] Water
- [ ] Water
- [ ] Water
- [ ] Go to sleep Happy!

Daily Calendar

5:00

6:00

7:00

8:00

9:00

10:00

11:00

12:00

1:00

2:00

3:00

4:00

5:00

6:00

7:00

8:00

9:00

Daily Focus

People to Contact

To Do Today

Gratitude

Personal
_____

Love & Relationships
_____

Professional
_____

Life
_____

#1 Priority to get me one step closer to achieving my main goal is:
_____

I am going to focus and improve on:
_____

Today is the first day of the rest of my beautiful life, what am I going to do to make a difference?
_____

Today is YOUR day and just by waking up it is already amazing!

Daily Reflection

Food Journal

Breakfast
Snack
Lunch
Snack
Dinner
Other

Exercise

RATE YOUR DAY

PERSONAL   LOVE   WORK   OVERALL

> The best way to do ourselves good is to do good to others. – Thomas Brooks

Daily To Do

- [ ] Wake up & smile
- [ ] Walk/Run
- [ ] Gratitude
- [ ] Read
- [ ] Meditate
- [ ] Make Bed
- [ ] Donate
- [ ] Exercise
- [ ] Stretch
- [ ] Learn
- [ ] Thank you
- [ ] Day Prep
- [ ] Journal
- [ ] Visualize
- [ ] Water
- [ ] Water
- [ ] Water
- [ ] Go to sleep Happy!

Daily Calendar

5:00
6:00
7:00
8:00
9:00
10:00
11:00
12:00
1:00
2:00
3:00
4:00
5:00
6:00
7:00
8:00
9:00

Daily Focus

People to Contact

To Do Today

Sunday

Today is your day to relax, regroup, reflect and prepare for the next amazing week!
What do you feel went really well this past week? List at least 5 accomplishments.

_____

_____

What would you like to improve on for this upcoming week?

_____

_____

What is ONE step that you will take this week to get closer to your dream?

_____

_____

Is there someone that could use your help this week? How can you make a difference?

_____

Weekly Challenge

The challenge this week is to organize your own fundraising event! Sounds like a lot of work, time and effort but it doesn't have to be.

You could do a neighbourhood bottle drive with your kids—let your neighbours know that you are donating the money from the drive to the local animal shelter and I'm sure they'd be happy to help. This only takes one Saturday afternoon (even less time if you phone ahead and let them know you're doing it).

You could host a dinner party with friends and family and ask that everyone bring a canned good or two for the local food bank. You could organize a coat drive at your children's school and get the kids involved too! There are many ways to give back that will make a huge difference in so many other lives all without putting too much of a strain on your schedule or wallet.

Who knows, maybe it will become an annual thing!

Goals for this week

Health and Fitness

Love and Relationship

Career and Finance

Philanthropy and Giving Back

Shopping list

Hint:
Take a look at your one-year and three-month goals. How can you get closer to achieving them?

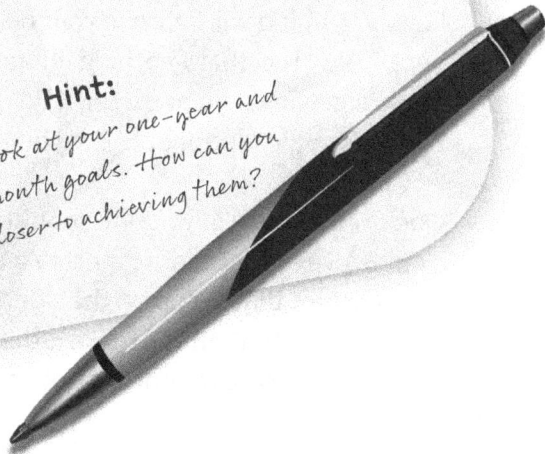

Career

Do you wake up every morning excited to start the day? Are you amped up to get to work and make a difference? It doesn't matter your position or what your job is at this very moment—do you still give it your best every day?

A huge portion of life is spent at work, whether it's a nine-to-five job, an online business, a home business … working for yourself, or working for someone else. Enjoying what you do is crucial if you want to be the ULTIMATE YOU! Doing something that fills your days and heart with pleasure is the best thing you can do to enhance other areas of your life too. If you love what you do, you generally wake up happy and it permeates your day. Of course, we all have our challenging days, but for the most part, if you are excited about the amazing things you get to accomplish, learn or share at your job, you are ahead of the game.

Loving your job means you wake up raring to go, are pleasant to be around, are happy with your spouse and/or kids first thing in the morning, enjoy your drive to work and spend the whole day changing the world (all changes, big or small, count—I truly believe every contribution matters). Then after work, because you are energized by having a positive day, you will still have a desire to play with your kids, exercise, enjoy a hobby or engage in a romantic evening with your spouse.

Loving your job will improve your health, your relationships, your intellect … there is no down side here. There is actually nothing but positives! And on top of all of that, if you love what you do, then you are getting paid to do something that you love! What? That sounds pretty dreamy, doesn't it? Well this could (and should) be your reality.

One primary goal in your life should be to find a career or create a business that makes your heart sing. However, sometimes this takes a little time and we still have responsibilities to take care of while we get that set up on the side. But there are many ways we can create that excitement about our current situation and make it the best experience possible (and by the laws of the universe, this will actually bring your dream job into fruition a lot faster).

Adjusting your attitude and really focusing on what you are bringing into the workplace is a great place to start. How about doing what you can to uplift and inspire others around you ... how can you make their day a little bit brighter? Or how about the people you get to serve throughout the day; can you make their day better?

It does not matter if you are making multi-million dollar decisions, flipping burgers, maintaining and keeping a school clean, picking flowers or raising kids—whatever your job is, do your very best and the very best will be returned back to you!

If you want to be your own boss, answer these questions and then take action:

- What am I good at?
- What do I love?
- What does the world need?
- How do I get paid?

The world is waiting for you to bring your passion to life, what are you waiting for?

Book Recommendations
High Performance Habits – Brendon Burchard
Eat that Frog – Brian Tracy

YouTube/Internet
Find Your True Gift and Maximise Your Career – Anthony Robbins

Affirmation
"I am so happy and grateful that I have attracted my dream career"

Gratitude

Personal
_____

Love & Relationships
_____

Professional
_____

Life
_____

#1 Priority to get me one step closer to achieving my main goal is:
_____

I am going to focus and improve on:
_____

Today is the first day of the rest of my beautiful life, what am I going to do to make a difference?
_____

Today is YOUR day and just by waking up it is already amazing!

Daily Reflection
_____
_____
_____
_____
_____
_____
_____
_____
_____
_____

Food Journal

Breakfast
Snack
Lunch
Snack
Dinner
Other

Exercise

RATE YOUR DAY

PERSONAL   LOVE   WORK   OVERALL

Daily To Do

- ☐ Wake up & smile
- ☐ Walk/Run
- ☐ Gratitude
- ☐ Read
- ☐ Meditate
- ☐ Make Bed
- ☐ Donate
- ☐ Exercise
- ☐ Stretch
- ☐ Learn
- ☐ Thank you
- ☐ Day Prep
- ☐ Journal
- ☐ Visualize
- ☐ Water
- ☐ Water
- ☐ Water
- ☐ Go to sleep Happy!

Daily Calendar

5:00

6:00

7:00

8:00

9:00

10:00

11:00

12:00

1:00

2:00

3:00

4:00

5:00

6:00

7:00

8:00

9:00

Daily Focus

People to Contact

To Do Today

Gratitude

Personal

_____

Love & Relationships

_____

Professional

_____

Life

_____

#1 Priority to get me one step closer to achieving my main goal is:

_____

I am going to focus and improve on:

_____

Today is the first day of the rest of my beautiful life, what am I going to do to make a difference?

_____

Daily Reflection

_____
_____
_____
_____
_____
_____
_____
_____
_____
_____
_____

Food Journal

Breakfast

Snack

Lunch

Snack

Dinner

Other

Exercise

RATE YOUR DAY

PERSONAL   LOVE   WORK   OVERALL

Daily To Do

- ☐ Wake up & smile
- ☐ Walk/Run
- ☐ Gratitude
- ☐ Read
- ☐ Meditate
- ☐ Make Bed
- ☐ Donate
- ☐ Exercise
- ☐ Stretch
- ☐ Learn
- ☐ Thank you
- ☐ Day Prep
- ☐ Journal
- ☐ Visualize
- ☐ Water
- ☐ Water
- ☐ Water
- ☐ Go to sleep Happy!

Daily Calendar

5:00

6:00

7:00

8:00

9:00

10:00

11:00

12:00

1:00

2:00

3:00

4:00

5:00

6:00

7:00

8:00

9:00

Daily Focus

People to Contact

To Do Today

Gratitude

Personal
_____

Love & Relationships
_____

Professional
_____

Life
_____

#1 Priority to get me one step closer to achieving my main goal is:
_____

I am going to focus and improve on:
_____

Today is the first day of the rest of my beautiful life, what am I going to do to make a difference?
_____

Daily Reflection

_____
_____
_____
_____
_____
_____
_____
_____
_____

Food Journal

Breakfast
Snack
Lunch
Snack
Dinner
Other

Exercise

RATE YOUR DAY

PERSONAL   LOVE   WORK   OVERALL

Whatever you decide to do, make sure it makes you happy.

Daily To Do

- [ ] Wake up & smile
- [ ] Walk/Run
- [ ] Gratitude
- [ ] Read
- [ ] Meditate
- [ ] Make Bed
- [ ] Donate
- [ ] Exercise
- [ ] Stretch
- [ ] Learn
- [ ] Thank you
- [ ] Day Prep
- [ ] Journal
- [ ] Visualize
- [ ] Water
- [ ] Water
- [ ] Water
- [ ] Go to sleep Happy!

Daily Calendar

5:00
6:00
7:00
8:00
9:00
10:00
11:00
12:00
1:00
2:00
3:00
4:00
5:00
6:00
7:00
8:00
9:00

Daily Focus

People to Contact

To Do Today

Gratitude

Personal
_____

Love & Relationships
_____

Professional
_____

Life
_____

#1 Priority to get me one step closer to achieving my main goal is:
_____

I am going to focus and improve on:
_____

Today is the first day of the rest of my beautiful life, what am I going to do to make a difference?
_____

Daily Reflection
_____
_____
_____
_____
_____
_____
_____
_____
_____
_____
_____
_____

Food Journal

Breakfast
Snack
Lunch
Snack
Dinner
Other

Exercise

RATE YOUR DAY

PERSONAL   LOVE   WORK   OVERALL

Daily To Do

- ☐ Wake up & smile
- ☐ Walk/Run
- ☐ Gratitude
- ☐ Read
- ☐ Meditate
- ☐ Make Bed
- ☐ Donate
- ☐ Exercise
- ☐ Stretch
- ☐ Learn
- ☐ Thank you
- ☐ Day Prep
- ☐ Journal
- ☐ Visualize
- ☐ Water
- ☐ Water
- ☐ Water
- ☐ Go to sleep Happy!

Daily Calendar

5:00

6:00

7:00

8:00

9:00

10:00

11:00

12:00

1:00

2:00

3:00

4:00

5:00

6:00

7:00

8:00

9:00

Daily Focus

People to Contact

To Do Today

Gratitude

Personal

_____

Love & Relationships

_____

Professional

_____

Life

_____

#1 Priority to get me one step closer to achieving my main goal is:

_____

I am going to focus and improve on:

_____

Today is the first day of the rest of my beautiful life, what am I going to do to make a difference?

_____

Today is YOUR day
and just by waking up
it is already amazing!

Daily Reflection

Food Journal

Breakfast

Snack

Lunch

Snack

Dinner

Other

Exercise

RATE YOUR DAY

PERSONAL   LOVE   WORK   OVERALL

> The future belongs to those who believe in the beauty of their dreams. - Eleanor Roosevelt

Daily To Do

- [ ] Wake up & smile
- [ ] Walk/Run
- [ ] Gratitude
- [ ] Read
- [ ] Meditate
- [ ] Make Bed
- [ ] Donate
- [ ] Exercise
- [ ] Stretch
- [ ] Learn
- [ ] Thank you
- [ ] Day Prep
- [ ] Journal
- [ ] Visualize
- [ ] Water
- [ ] Water
- [ ] Water
- [ ] Go to sleep Happy!

Daily Calendar

5:00
6:00
7:00
8:00
9:00
10:00
11:00
12:00
1:00
2:00
3:00
4:00
5:00
6:00
7:00
8:00
9:00

Daily Focus

People to Contact

To Do Today

Gratitude

Personal

Love & Relationships

Professional

Life

#1 Priority to get me one step closer to achieving my main goal is:

I am going to focus and improve on:

Today is the first day of the rest of my beautiful life, what am I going to do to make a difference?

Daily Reflection

Food Journal

Breakfast

Snack

Lunch

Snack

Dinner

Other

Exercise

RATE YOUR DAY

PERSONAL   LOVE   WORK   OVERALL

Daily To Do

- [ ] Wake up & smile
- [ ] Walk/Run
- [ ] Gratitude
- [ ] Read
- [ ] Meditate
- [ ] Make Bed
- [ ] Donate
- [ ] Exercise
- [ ] Stretch
- [ ] Learn
- [ ] Thank you
- [ ] Day Prep
- [ ] Journal
- [ ] Visualize
- [ ] Water
- [ ] Water
- [ ] Water
- [ ] Go to sleep Happy!

Daily Calendar

5:00

6:00

7:00

8:00

9:00

10:00

11:00

12:00

1:00

2:00

3:00

4:00

5:00

6:00

7:00

8:00

9:00

Daily Focus

People to Contact

To Do Today

Gratitude

Personal
_____

Love & Relationships
_____

Professional
_____

Life
_____

#1 Priority to get me one step closer to achieving my main goal is:
_____

I am going to focus and improve on:
_____

Today is the first day of the rest of my beautiful life, what am I going to do to make a difference?
_____

Daily Reflection

Food Journal

Breakfast _____
Snack _____
Lunch _____
Snack _____
Dinner _____
Other _____

Exercise

RATE YOUR DAY

PERSONAL   LOVE   WORK   OVERALL

Daily To Do

- [ ] Wake up & smile
- [ ] Walk/Run
- [ ] Gratitude
- [ ] Read
- [ ] Meditate
- [ ] Make Bed
- [ ] Donate
- [ ] Exercise
- [ ] Stretch
- [ ] Learn
- [ ] Thank you
- [ ] Day Prep
- [ ] Journal
- [ ] Visualize
- [ ] Water
- [ ] Water
- [ ] Water
- [ ] Go to sleep Happy!

Daily Calendar

5:00

6:00

7:00

8:00

9:00

10:00

11:00

12:00

1:00

2:00

3:00

4:00

5:00

6:00

7:00

8:00

9:00

Daily Focus

People to Contact

To Do Today

Sunday

Today is your day to relax, regroup, reflect and prepare for the next amazing week!
What do you feel went really well this past week? List at least 5 accomplishments.

_____

_____

What would you like to improve on for this upcoming week?

_____

_____

What is ONE step that you will take this week to get closer to your dream?

_____

_____

Is there someone that could use your help this week? How can you make a difference?

_____

Weekly Challenge 1

Double Time! We are amping it up — 2 challenges

Work when at work, play when at play.

The challenge this week is to clear all distractions from your mind and really focus when you are at work. Whether you work at an office or in the field, for yourself or a big company, when you are at work, make sure you are completely present. If you work at a desk, clear everything off it that you're not working on. Close down the email/ social media pages and the news site and pay attention to the task at hand.

If you were to track the amount of hours you actually work while at your job, you might be a little shocked to find how much time gets wasted. Imagine how productive you could be if all your time was focused on a prioritized list of things to do! You would be knocking the important things off your list like crazy; you feel so accomplished, happy, energetic and proud.

Weekly Challenge 2

Give yourself the energy boost and body breaks you need to remain a task-accomplishing star all day long!

The challenge this week is to set an alarm on your phone to go off every hour as a reminder for you to get up and stretch, take some deep breaths, fill up your water bottle, smile at your colleagues (if you have them) and get pumped for the rest of the next hour.

The afternoon slump can be a tough one, but getting up to take a short walk and moving around to shake things up have all have been proven to create a huge positive effect on mental and physical stamina.

Goals for this week

Health and Fitness

Love and Relationship

Career and Finance

Philanthropy and Giving Back

Hint:
Take a look at your one-year and
three-month goals. How can you
get closer to achieving them?

Shopping list

Gratitude

Personal
_____

Love & Relationships
_____

Professional
_____

Life
_____

#1 Priority to get me one step closer to achieving my main goal is:
_____

I am going to focus and improve on:
_____

Today is the first day of the rest of my beautiful life, what am I going to do to make a difference?
_____

Daily Reflection

_____
_____
_____
_____
_____
_____
_____
_____
_____
_____

Food Journal

Breakfast	
Snack	
Lunch	
Snack	
Dinner	
Other	

Exercise

RATE YOUR DAY

PERSONAL   LOVE   WORK   OVERALL

Daily To Do

- [ ] Wake up & smile
- [ ] Walk/Run
- [ ] Gratitude
- [ ] Read
- [ ] Meditate
- [ ] Make Bed
- [ ] Donate
- [ ] Exercise
- [ ] Stretch
- [ ] Learn
- [ ] Thank you
- [ ] Day Prep
- [ ] Journal
- [ ] Visualize
- [ ] Water
- [ ] Water
- [ ] Water
- [ ] Go to sleep Happy!

Daily Calendar

5:00

6:00

7:00

8:00

9:00

10:00

11:00

12:00

1:00

2:00

3:00

4:00

5:00

6:00

7:00

8:00

9:00

Daily Focus

People to Contact

To Do Today

Gratitude

Personal

Love & Relationships

Professional

Life

#1 Priority to get me one step closer to achieving my main goal is:

I am going to focus and improve on:

Today is the first day of the rest of my beautiful life, what am I going to do to make a difference?

Daily Reflection

Food Journal

Breakfast

Snack

Lunch

Snack

Dinner

Other

Exercise

RATE YOUR DAY

PERSONAL   LOVE   WORK   OVERALL

Daily To Do

- [ ] Wake up & smile
- [ ] Walk/Run
- [ ] Gratitude
- [ ] Read
- [ ] Meditate
- [ ] Make Bed
- [ ] Donate
- [ ] Exercise
- [ ] Stretch
- [ ] Learn
- [ ] Thank you
- [ ] Day Prep
- [ ] Journal
- [ ] Visualize
- [ ] Water
- [ ] Water
- [ ] Water
- [ ] Go to sleep Happy!

Daily Calendar

5:00

6:00

7:00

8:00

9:00

10:00

11:00

12:00

1:00

2:00

3:00

4:00

5:00

6:00

7:00

8:00

9:00

Daily Focus

People to Contact

To Do Today

Gratitude

Personal
_____

Love & Relationships
_____

Professional
_____

Life
_____

#1 Priority to get me one step closer to achieving my main goal is:
_____

I am going to focus and improve on:
_____

Today is the first day of the rest of my beautiful life, what am I going to do to make a difference?
_____

Daily Reflection

Food Journal

Breakfast
Snack
Lunch
Snack
Dinner
Other

Exercise

RATE YOUR DAY

PERSONAL   LOVE   WORK   OVERALL

Daily To Do

- ☐ Wake up & smile
- ☐ Walk/Run
- ☐ Gratitude
- ☐ Read
- ☐ Meditate
- ☐ Make Bed
- ☐ Donate
- ☐ Exercise
- ☐ Stretch
- ☐ Learn
- ☐ Thank you
- ☐ Day Prep
- ☐ Journal
- ☐ Visualize
- ☐ Water
- ☐ Water
- ☐ Water
- ☐ Go to sleep Happy!

Daily Calendar

5:00
6:00
7:00
8:00
9:00
10:00
11:00
12:00
1:00
2:00
3:00
4:00
5:00
6:00
7:00
8:00
9:00

Daily Focus

People to Contact

To Do Today

Gratitude

Personal
_____

Love & Relationships
_____

Professional
_____

Life
_____

#1 Priority to get me one step closer to achieving my main goal is:
_____

I am going to focus and improve on:
_____

Today is the first day of the rest of my beautiful life, what am I going to do to make a difference?
_____

Today is YOUR day
and just by waking up
it is already amazing!

Daily Reflection
_____
_____
_____
_____
_____
_____
_____
_____
_____
_____

Food Journal

Breakfast
Snack
Lunch
Snack
Dinner
Other

Exercise

RATE YOUR DAY

PERSONAL   LOVE   WORK   OVERALL

If opportunity doesn't knock - BUILD A DOOR. - Milton Berle

Daily To Do

- [ ] Wake up & smile
- [ ] Walk/Run
- [ ] Gratitude
- [ ] Read
- [ ] Meditate
- [ ] Make Bed
- [ ] Donate
- [ ] Exercise
- [ ] Stretch
- [ ] Learn
- [ ] Thank you
- [ ] Day Prep
- [ ] Journal
- [ ] Visualize
- [ ] Water
- [ ] Water
- [ ] Water
- [ ] Go to sleep Happy!

Daily Calendar

5:00
6:00
7:00
8:00
9:00
10:00
11:00
12:00
1:00
2:00
3:00
4:00
5:00
6:00
7:00
8:00
9:00

Daily Focus

People to Contact

To Do Today

Gratitude

Personal
_____

Love & Relationships
_____

Professional
_____

Life
_____

#1 Priority to get me one step closer to achieving my main goal is:
_____

I am going to focus and improve on:
_____

Today is the first day of the rest of my beautiful life, what am I going to do to make a difference?
_____

Daily Reflection
_____
_____
_____
_____
_____
_____
_____
_____
_____
_____

Food Journal

Breakfast
Snack
Lunch
Snack
Dinner
Other

Exercise

RATE YOUR DAY

PERSONAL   LOVE   WORK   OVERALL

Daily To Do

- [ ] Wake up & smile
- [ ] Walk/Run
- [ ] Gratitude
- [ ] Read
- [ ] Meditate
- [ ] Make Bed
- [ ] Donate
- [ ] Exercise
- [ ] Stretch
- [ ] Learn
- [ ] Thank you
- [ ] Day Prep
- [ ] Journal
- [ ] Visualize
- [ ] Water
- [ ] Water
- [ ] Water
- [ ] Go to sleep Happy!

Daily Calendar

5:00

6:00

7:00

8:00

9:00

10:00

11:00

12:00

1:00

2:00

3:00

4:00

5:00

6:00

7:00

8:00

9:00

Daily Focus

People to Contact

To Do Today

Gratitude

Personal

_____

Love & Relationships

_____

Professional

_____

Life

_____

#1 Priority to get me one step closer to achieving my main goal is:

_____

I am going to focus and improve on:

_____

Today is the first day of the rest of my beautiful life, what am I going to do to make a difference?

_____

Today is YOUR day and just by waking up it is already amazing!

Daily Reflection

_____
_____
_____
_____
_____
_____
_____
_____
_____
_____
_____

Food Journal

Breakfast

Snack

Lunch

Snack

Dinner

Other

Exercise

RATE YOUR DAY

PERSONAL   LOVE   WORK   OVERALL

If your dreams don't scare you, they aren't big enough!

Saturday

Daily To Do

- [ ] Wake up & smile
- [ ] Walk/Run
- [ ] Gratitude
- [ ] Read
- [ ] Meditate
- [ ] Make Bed
- [ ] Donate
- [ ] Exercise
- [ ] Stretch
- [ ] Learn
- [ ] Thank you
- [ ] Day Prep
- [ ] Journal
- [ ] Visualize
- [ ] Water
- [ ] Water
- [ ] Water
- [ ] Go to sleep Happy!

Daily Calendar

5:00
6:00
7:00
8:00
9:00
10:00
11:00
12:00
1:00
2:00
3:00
4:00
5:00
6:00
7:00
8:00
9:00

Daily Focus

People to Contact

To Do Today

Gratitude

Personal
_____

Love & Relationships
_____

Professional
_____

Life
_____

#1 Priority to get me one step closer to achieving my main goal is:
_____

I am going to focus and improve on:
_____

Today is the first day of the rest of my beautiful life, what am I going to do to make a difference?
_____

Today is YOUR day
and just by waking up
it is already amazing!

Daily Reflection

Food Journal

Breakfast
Snack
Lunch
Snack
Dinner
Other

Exercise

RATE YOUR DAY

PERSONAL   LOVE   WORK   OVERALL

Daily To Do

- [ ] Wake up & smile
- [ ] Walk/Run
- [ ] Gratitude
- [ ] Read
- [ ] Meditate
- [ ] Make Bed
- [ ] Donate
- [ ] Exercise
- [ ] Stretch
- [ ] Learn
- [ ] Thank you
- [ ] Day Prep
- [ ] Journal
- [ ] Visualize
- [ ] Water
- [ ] Water
- [ ] Water
- [ ] Go to sleep Happy!

Daily Calendar

5:00

6:00

7:00

8:00

9:00

10:00

11:00

12:00

1:00

2:00

3:00

4:00

5:00

6:00

7:00

8:00

9:00

Daily Focus

People to Contact

To Do Today

Sunday

Today is your day to relax, regroup, reflect and prepare for the next amazing week! What do you feel went really well this past week? List at least 5 accomplishments.

_____

_____

What would you like to improve on for this upcoming week?

_____

_____

What is ONE step that you will take this week to get closer to your dream?

_____

_____

Is there someone that could use your help this week? How can you make a difference?

_____

Weekly Challenge 1

Always give more then you hope to receive: The challenge this week is to give the very best of yourself in every situation.

Even if you are in a temporary job or career; even if you are building your dream job on the side—really focus and know with all your heart that at the end of every day you have left no stone unturned.

- During your meetings be there, be involved and YOU give everything you have.
- Take the time to read and answer emails carefully.
- When you deal with customers you listen carefully and hear exactly what it is that they need from you.

If you do these things, you will be able to provide the best possible service.

Weekly Challenge 2

Give your best and the best will be given to you!

We spend a third of our life at our place of work, so let's make it the best possible atmosphere we can. The challenge this week is two-part:

- First, only speak kind words—don't get involved in workplace gossip. If it starts around you, excuse yourself from the situation, change the topic or, if you feel comfortable enough to say so, let the others know you have hopes for a positive work environment that doesn't include gossip.
- Second, do something to uplift your colleagues: bring in a treat, celebrate a successful day, suggest after-work get-together, play some happy music or compliment people! Do whatever you can to spread some good vibes!

Goals for this week

Health and Fitness

Love and Relationship

Career and Finance

Philanthropy and Giving Back

Shopping list

Hint:
Take a look at your one-year and three-month goals. How can you get closer to achieving them?

Finances

Let's focus on your abundant finances! Specifically, how to organize your wallet, papers and debts—get set up on a regular repayment plan and then forget about them!

Focusing on the abundance you already have in your life and the amount that you would LIKE to see in your account is way more beneficial than reminding yourself about any mound of debt you have. Remember, you attract what you think about! What you put out into the universal consciousness is what you will get back, so constantly send out rich, abundant thoughts, speak positive words and act in honorable ways.

Like everything else in the world, money is just energy. This is amazing because it means that as soon as we get on the same frequency as money we will attract it into our lives at a substantial rate. The reason this is so amazing is because money makes life better. Money can absolutely solve problems. Money is awesome. Just as love, positive thinking and complete health can change your life, so can money!

Close your eyes and picture this: imagine that everywhere you look, you see beauty! You spend countless hours just being grateful for all the amazing people and things you have in your life. You have the ability to turn a 'bad' situation into something to learn and grow from. You are so in love and surrounded by love that your heart is overflowing. You have a strong, healthy, sexy body and your bank account is abundant, which allows you to build your dream home, take beautiful vacations with your family, start your dream business, pursue your hobbies, help friends and family and give back to your community and the world in huge ways.

Some of this is absolutely possible without money but I can guarantee money makes it easier. Money can buy a gym membership, healthy foods and water to nourish the body. Money puts a roof over your head where you are comfortable and safe. Money buys you a car, bike or bus pass to get to and from work. Money enables your kids to try out new sports, musical instruments and take family vacations. Money buys books and tickets to seminars where you feed your intellectual health, meet likeminded people and learn how to accomplish your goals.

This could go on for pages—money is just so great and I wrote this book to hopefully show you that it is an excellent thing to have money. Having an abundance of money is your birthright. A lot of people, without even knowing it, are blocking their own flow of abundance because they focus on the poverty that is around the world and then tell themselves they don't deserve it, saying out loud or to themselves, "Who am I to have a beautiful, fulfilled life and full bank account?" Or maybe they say, "I don't need money to be happy," or they know of a person who has money and is a jerk so they believe and tell others that, "Rich people are stuck up."

Don't believe these things! All of these statements will only hurt you. I promise that you can make more of a difference in the world if you have money!

A great quote about money is, "Money doesn't change people; it only enhances who they truly are." I love this! When you see people driving fancy cars, living in beautiful home(s), traveling the world and living life to the fullest, it is important to be happy for them! Jealousy and resentment only push those same riches further away from you. Be thrilled about their success and know that this level of success being in your life is not far off.

Something really important to remember is that money on its own doesn't have any power; you give it power when you decide what you want to do with it. Whether you are using it for necessities—like having a roof over your head, food in the fridge, fresh water to drink and clothing to wear—or you are using money to enrich the lives of others, better the planet or invent something that is going to change life as we know it, money is just paper until you turn it into something more.

Book Recommendation
Rich Dad, Poor Dad – Robert T. Kiyosaki

YouTube/ Internet
Neuro-gym – John Assaraf

Affirmation
"I have more than enough money to spare and share."

Gratitude

Personal

_____

Love & Relationships

_____

Professional

_____

Life

_____

#1 Priority to get me one step closer to achieving my main goal is:

_____

I am going to focus and improve on:

_____

Today is the first day of the rest of my beautiful life, what am I going to do to make a difference?

_____

Daily Reflection

_____
_____
_____
_____
_____
_____
_____
_____
_____
_____
_____
_____
_____

Food Journal

Breakfast

Snack

Lunch

Snack

Dinner

Other

Exercise

RATE YOUR DAY

PERSONAL   LOVE   WORK   OVERALL

Everybody is a genius. But if you judge a fish by it's ability to climb a tree it will live it's whole life believing it's stupid. - Albert Einstein

Monday

Daily To Do

- [ ] Wake up & smile
- [ ] Walk/Run
- [ ] Gratitude
- [ ] Read
- [ ] Meditate
- [ ] Make Bed
- [ ] Donate
- [ ] Exercise
- [ ] Stretch
- [ ] Learn
- [ ] Thank you
- [ ] Day Prep
- [ ] Journal
- [ ] Visualize
- [ ] Water
- [ ] Water
- [ ] Water
- [ ] Go to sleep Happy!

Daily Calendar

5:00
6:00
7:00
8:00
9:00
10:00
11:00
12:00
1:00
2:00
3:00
4:00
5:00
6:00
7:00
8:00
9:00

Daily Focus

People to Contact

To Do Today

Gratitude

Personal

Love & Relationships

Professional

Life

#1 Priority to get me one step closer to achieving my main goal is:

I am going to focus and improve on:

Today is the first day of the rest of my beautiful life, what am I going to do to make a difference?

Daily Reflection

Food Journal

Breakfast

Snack

Lunch

Snack

Dinner

Other

Exercise

RATE YOUR DAY

PERSONAL   LOVE   WORK   OVERALL

For things to change - you have to change. For things to be different - you must be different. Before financial success can occur, personal growth must occur. - Jim Rohn

Tuesday

Daily To Do

- [ ] Wake up & smile
- [ ] Walk/Run
- [ ] Gratitude
- [ ] Read
- [ ] Meditate
- [ ] Make Bed
- [ ] Donate
- [ ] Exercise
- [ ] Stretch
- [ ] Learn
- [ ] Thank you
- [ ] Day Prep
- [ ] Journal
- [ ] Visualize
- [ ] Water
- [ ] Water
- [ ] Water
- [ ] Go to sleep Happy!

Daily Calendar

5:00

6:00

7:00

8:00

9:00

10:00

11:00

12:00

1:00

2:00

3:00

4:00

5:00

6:00

7:00

8:00

9:00

Daily Focus

People to Contact

To Do Today

Gratitude

Personal

Love & Relationships

Professional

Life

#1 Priority to get me one step closer to achieving my main goal is:

I am going to focus and improve on:

Today is the first day of the rest of my beautiful life, what am I going to do to make a difference?

Daily Reflection

Food Journal

Breakfast

Snack

Lunch

Snack

Dinner

Other

Exercise

RATE YOUR DAY

PERSONAL   LOVE   WORK   OVERALL

Daily To Do

- ☐ Wake up & smile
- ☐ Walk/Run
- ☐ Gratitude
- ☐ Read
- ☐ Meditate
- ☐ Make Bed
- ☐ Donate
- ☐ Exercise
- ☐ Stretch
- ☐ Learn
- ☐ Thank you
- ☐ Day Prep
- ☐ Journal
- ☐ Visualize
- ☐ Water
- ☐ Water
- ☐ Water
- ☐ Go to sleep Happy!

Daily Calendar

5:00

6:00

7:00

8:00

9:00

10:00

11:00

12:00

1:00

2:00

3:00

4:00

5:00

6:00

7:00

8:00

9:00

Daily Focus

People to Contact

To Do Today

Gratitude

Personal
_____

Love & Relationships
_____

Professional
_____

Life
_____

#1 Priority to get me one step closer to achieving my main goal is:
_____

I am going to focus and improve on:
_____

Today is the first day of the rest of my beautiful life, what am I going to do to make a difference?
_____

Daily Reflection
_____
_____
_____
_____
_____
_____
_____
_____
_____
_____

Food Journal

Breakfast _____
Snack _____
Lunch _____
Snack _____
Dinner _____
Other _____

Exercise
_____
_____

RATE YOUR DAY

PERSONAL   LOVE   WORK   OVERALL

The goal isn't more money - it's living life on your terms.- Chris Brogan

Daily To Do

- [ ] Wake up & smile
- [ ] Walk/Run
- [ ] Gratitude
- [ ] Read
- [ ] Meditate
- [ ] Make Bed
- [ ] Donate
- [ ] Exercise
- [ ] Stretch
- [ ] Learn
- [ ] Thank you
- [ ] Day Prep
- [ ] Journal
- [ ] Visualize
- [ ] Water
- [ ] Water
- [ ] Water
- [ ] Go to sleep Happy!

Daily Calendar

5:00

6:00

7:00

8:00

9:00

10:00

11:00

12:00

1:00

2:00

3:00

4:00

5:00

6:00

7:00

8:00

9:00

Daily Focus

People to Contact

To Do Today

Gratitude

Personal

_____

Love & Relationships

_____

Professional

_____

Life

_____

#1 Priority to get me one step closer to achieving my main goal is:

_____

I am going to focus and improve on:

_____

Today is the first day of the rest of my beautiful life, what am I going to do to make a difference?

_____

Today is YOUR day and just by waking up it is already amazing!

Daily Reflection

_____
_____
_____
_____
_____
_____
_____
_____
_____
_____
_____
_____

Food Journal

Breakfast
Snack
Lunch
Snack
Dinner
Other

Exercise

RATE YOUR DAY

PERSONAL   LOVE   WORK   OVERALL

Daily To Do

- ☐ Wake up & smile
- ☐ Walk/Run
- ☐ Gratitude
- ☐ Read
- ☐ Meditate
- ☐ Make Bed
- ☐ Donate
- ☐ Exercise
- ☐ Stretch
- ☐ Learn
- ☐ Thank you
- ☐ Day Prep
- ☐ Journal
- ☐ Visualize
- ☐ Water
- ☐ Water
- ☐ Water
- ☐ Go to sleep Happy!

Daily Calendar

5:00

6:00

7:00

8:00

9:00

10:00

11:00

12:00

1:00

2:00

3:00

4:00

5:00

6:00

7:00

8:00

9:00

Daily Focus

People to Contact

To Do Today

Gratitude

Personal

_____

Love & Relationships

_____

Professional

_____

Life

_____

#1 Priority to get me one step closer to achieving my main goal is:

_____

I am going to focus and improve on:

_____

Today is the first day of the rest of my beautiful life, what am I going to do to make a difference?

_____

Daily Reflection

Food Journal

Breakfast

Snack

Lunch

Snack

Dinner

Other

Exercise

RATE YOUR DAY

PERSONAL   LOVE   WORK   OVERALL

Saturday

Daily To Do

- ☐ Wake up & smile
- ☐ Walk/Run
- ☐ Gratitude
- ☐ Read
- ☐ Meditate
- ☐ Make Bed
- ☐ Donate
- ☐ Exercise
- ☐ Stretch
- ☐ Learn
- ☐ Thank you
- ☐ Day Prep
- ☐ Journal
- ☐ Visualize
- ☐ Water
- ☐ Water
- ☐ Water
- ☐ Go to sleep Happy!

Daily Calendar

5:00

6:00

7:00

8:00

9:00

10:00

11:00

12:00

1:00

2:00

3:00

4:00

5:00

6:00

7:00

8:00

9:00

Daily Focus

People to Contact

To Do Today

Gratitude

Personal
_____

Love & Relationships
_____

Professional
_____

Life
_____

#1 Priority to get me one step closer to achieving my main goal is:
_____

I am going to focus and improve on:
_____

Today is the first day of the rest of my beautiful life, what am I going to do to make a difference?
_____

Daily Reflection
_____
_____
_____
_____
_____
_____
_____
_____
_____
_____

Food Journal

Breakfast _____
Snack _____
Lunch _____
Snack _____
Dinner _____
Other _____

Exercise
_____
_____

RATE YOUR DAY

PERSONAL   LOVE   WORK   OVERALL

80% of millionaires are self made- meaning they started with nothing but ambition and energy, something we all can have.

Daily To Do

- ☐ Wake up & smile
- ☐ Walk/Run
- ☐ Gratitude
- ☐ Read
- ☐ Meditate
- ☐ Make Bed
- ☐ Donate
- ☐ Exercise
- ☐ Stretch
- ☐ Learn
- ☐ Thank you
- ☐ Day Prep
- ☐ Journal
- ☐ Visualize
- ☐ Water
- ☐ Water
- ☐ Water
- ☐ Go to sleep Happy!

Daily Calendar

5:00

6:00

7:00

8:00

9:00

10:00

11:00

12:00

1:00

2:00

3:00

4:00

5:00

6:00

7:00

8:00

9:00

Daily Focus

People to Contact

To Do Today

Sunday

Today is your day to relax, regroup, reflect and prepare for the next amazing week!
What do you feel went really well this past week? List at least 5 accomplishments.

_____

_____

What would you like to improve on for this upcoming week?

_____

_____

What is ONE step that you will take this week to get closer to your dream?

_____

_____

Is there someone that could use your help this week? How can you make a difference?

_____

Weekly Challenge 1

The best savings plan is an automatic one! The same goes for debt repayment. Remember that energy flows where attention goes and results show—so if every month you are sitting down with a stack of bills trying to figure out which one to pay, or how much to pay on each, that's a pretty constant reminder.

The challenge this week is to work out a repayment plan for your debts and make it an automatic withdrawal from your account so that you can focus your time and energy on making the money! Also, set up an automatic savings plan. A great start is a tax free savings account where you just auto-transfer $25.00/ month (or whatever you are comfortable with) then sit back and watch your money pile up!

If you get some money you weren't expecting, throw it in there too! Looking at your bank account and seeing money is fabulous.

Weekly Challenge 2

Knowing you have money in your bank account is a fabulous feeling. Having goals and an action plan and writing them down makes your dreams 42 percent more likely to come true.

The challenge this week is to decide what your savings goal is, write it down, make a plan to achieve it and then take action.

For example: Say you want $2,500.00 in your account by the end of the year. Say there are eight months left in the year, so $2,500/8(months) = $312.50/month to save (or approximately $10.50) a day to reach your goal.

Once you have stated and written your goal and your achievable action plan, commit to it.

Goals for this week

Health and Fitness

Love and Relationship

Career and Finance

Philanthropy and Giving Back

Shopping list

Hint:
Take a look at your one-year and three-month goals. How can you get closer to achieving them?

Gratitude

Personal

_____

Love & Relationships

_____

Professional

_____

Life

_____

#1 Priority to get me one step closer to achieving my main goal is:

_____

I am going to focus and improve on:

_____

Today is the first day of the rest of my beautiful life, what am I going to do to make a difference?

_____

Daily Reflection

Food Journal

Breakfast

Snack

Lunch

Snack

Dinner

Other

Exercise

RATE YOUR DAY

PERSONAL   LOVE   WORK   OVERALL

Rich people act in spite of fear, Poor people let fear stop them.- T. Harv Eker

Daily To Do

- [ ] Wake up & smile
- [ ] Walk/Run
- [ ] Gratitude
- [ ] Read
- [ ] Meditate
- [ ] Make Bed
- [ ] Donate
- [ ] Exercise
- [ ] Stretch
- [ ] Learn
- [ ] Thank you
- [ ] Day Prep
- [ ] Journal
- [ ] Visualize
- [ ] Water
- [ ] Water
- [ ] Water
- [ ] Go to sleep Happy!

Daily Calendar

5:00

6:00

7:00

8:00

9:00

10:00

11:00

12:00

1:00

2:00

3:00

4:00

5:00

6:00

7:00

8:00

9:00

Daily Focus

People to Contact

To Do Today

Gratitude

Personal

_____

Love & Relationships

_____

Professional

_____

Life

_____

#1 Priority to get me one step closer to achieving my main goal is:

_____

I am going to focus and improve on:

_____

Today is the first day of the rest of my beautiful life, what am I going to do to make a difference?

_____

Today is YOUR day and just by waking up it is already amazing!

Daily Reflection

Food Journal

Breakfast _____
Snack _____
Lunch _____
Snack _____
Dinner _____
Other _____

Exercise

_____
_____

RATE YOUR DAY

PERSONAL   LOVE   WORK   OVERALL

Daily To Do

- [ ] Wake up & smile
- [ ] Walk/Run
- [ ] Gratitude
- [ ] Read
- [ ] Meditate
- [ ] Make Bed
- [ ] Donate
- [ ] Exercise
- [ ] Stretch
- [ ] Learn
- [ ] Thank you
- [ ] Day Prep
- [ ] Journal
- [ ] Visualize
- [ ] Water
- [ ] Water
- [ ] Water
- [ ] Go to sleep Happy!

Daily Calendar

5:00

6:00

7:00

8:00

9:00

10:00

11:00

12:00

1:00

2:00

3:00

4:00

5:00

6:00

7:00

8:00

9:00

Daily Focus

People to Contact

To Do Today

Gratitude

Personal
_____

Love & Relationships
_____

Professional
_____

Life
_____

#1 Priority to get me one step closer to achieving my main goal is:
_____

I am going to focus and improve on:
_____

Today is the first day of the rest of my beautiful life, what am I going to do to make a difference?
_____

Daily Reflection
_____
_____
_____
_____
_____
_____
_____
_____
_____
_____
_____

Food Journal

Breakfast
Snack
Lunch
Snack
Dinner
Other

Exercise

RATE YOUR DAY

PERSONAL   LOVE   WORK   OVERALL

Daily To Do

- ☐ Wake up & smile
- ☐ Walk/Run
- ☐ Gratitude
- ☐ Read
- ☐ Meditate
- ☐ Make Bed
- ☐ Donate
- ☐ Exercise
- ☐ Stretch
- ☐ Learn
- ☐ Thank you
- ☐ Day Prep
- ☐ Journal
- ☐ Visualize
- ☐ Water
- ☐ Water
- ☐ Water
- ☐ Go to sleep Happy!

Daily Calendar

5:00

6:00

7:00

8:00

9:00

10:00

11:00

12:00

1:00

2:00

3:00

4:00

5:00

6:00

7:00

8:00

9:00

Daily Focus

People to Contact

To Do Today

Gratitude

Personal
_____

Love & Relationships
_____

Professional
_____

Life
_____

#1 Priority to get me one step closer to achieving my main goal is:
_____

I am going to focus and improve on:
_____

Today is the first day of the rest of my beautiful life, what am I going to do to make a difference?
_____

Daily Reflection

Food Journal

Breakfast
Snack
Lunch
Snack
Dinner
Other

Exercise

RATE YOUR DAY

PERSONAL   LOVE   WORK   OVERALL

Thursday

Daily To Do

- ☐ Wake up & smile
- ☐ Walk/Run
- ☐ Gratitude
- ☐ Read
- ☐ Meditate
- ☐ Make Bed
- ☐ Donate
- ☐ Exercise
- ☐ Stretch
- ☐ Learn
- ☐ Thank you
- ☐ Day Prep
- ☐ Journal
- ☐ Visualize
- ☐ Water
- ☐ Water
- ☐ Water
- ☐ Go to sleep Happy!

Daily Calendar

5:00

6:00

7:00

8:00

9:00

10:00

11:00

12:00

1:00

2:00

3:00

4:00

5:00

6:00

7:00

8:00

9:00

Daily Focus

People to Contact

To Do Today

Gratitude

Personal
_____

Love & Relationships
_____

Professional
_____

Life
_____

#1 Priority to get me one step closer to achieving my main goal is:
_____

I am going to focus and improve on:
_____

Today is the first day of the rest of my beautiful life, what am I going to do to make a difference?
_____

Daily Reflection

Food Journal

Breakfast
Snack
Lunch
Snack
Dinner
Other

Exercise

RATE YOUR DAY

PERSONAL   LOVE   WORK   OVERALL

You are a money magnet.

Daily To Do

- [ ] Wake up & smile
- [ ] Walk/Run
- [ ] Gratitude
- [ ] Read
- [ ] Meditate
- [ ] Make Bed
- [ ] Donate
- [ ] Exercise
- [ ] Stretch
- [ ] Learn
- [ ] Thank you
- [ ] Day Prep
- [ ] Journal
- [ ] Visualize
- [ ] Water
- [ ] Water
- [ ] Water
- [ ] Go to sleep Happy!

Daily Calendar

5:00
6:00
7:00
8:00
9:00
10:00
11:00
12:00
1:00
2:00
3:00
4:00
5:00
6:00
7:00
8:00
9:00

Daily Focus

People to Contact

To Do Today

Gratitude

Personal

_____

Love & Relationships

_____

Professional

_____

Life

_____

#1 Priority to get me one step closer to achieving my main goal is:

_____

I am going to focus and improve on:

_____

Today is the first day of the rest of my beautiful life, what am I going to do to make a difference?

_____

Daily Reflection

_____

_____

_____

_____

_____

_____

_____

_____

Food Journal

Breakfast

Snack

Lunch

Snack

Dinner

Other

Exercise

RATE YOUR DAY

PERSONAL   LOVE   WORK   OVERALL

> **The price of anything is the amount of life you have to exchange for it. - Henry Thoreau**

Daily To Do

- ☐ Wake up & smile
- ☐ Walk/Run
- ☐ Gratitude
- ☐ Read
- ☐ Meditate
- ☐ Make Bed
- ☐ Donate
- ☐ Exercise
- ☐ Stretch
- ☐ Learn
- ☐ Thank you
- ☐ Day Prep
- ☐ Journal
- ☐ Visualize
- ☐ Water
- ☐ Water
- ☐ Water
- ☐ Go to sleep Happy!

Daily Calendar

5:00
6:00
7:00
8:00
9:00
10:00
11:00
12:00
1:00
2:00
3:00
4:00
5:00
6:00
7:00
8:00
9:00

Daily Focus

People to Contact

To Do Today

Gratitude

Personal

_____

Love & Relationships

_____

Professional

_____

Life

_____

#1 Priority to get me one step closer to achieving my main goal is:

_____

I am going to focus and improve on:

_____

Today is the first day of the rest of my beautiful life, what am I going to do to make a difference?

_____

Today is YOUR day and just by waking up it is already amazing!

Daily Reflection

Food Journal

Breakfast

Snack

Lunch

Snack

Dinner

Other

Exercise

RATE YOUR DAY

PERSONAL   LOVE   WORK   OVERALL

Daily To Do

- [ ] Wake up & smile
- [ ] Walk/Run
- [ ] Gratitude
- [ ] Read
- [ ] Meditate
- [ ] Make Bed
- [ ] Donate
- [ ] Exercise
- [ ] Stretch
- [ ] Learn
- [ ] Thank you
- [ ] Day Prep
- [ ] Journal
- [ ] Visualize
- [ ] Water
- [ ] Water
- [ ] Water
- [ ] Go to sleep Happy!

Daily Calendar

5:00

6:00

7:00

8:00

9:00

10:00

11:00

12:00

1:00

2:00

3:00

4:00

5:00

6:00

7:00

8:00

9:00

Daily Focus

People to Contact

To Do Today

Sunday

Today is your day to relax, regroup, reflect and prepare for the next amazing week!
What do you feel went really well this past week? List at least 5 accomplishments.

_____

_____

What would you like to improve on for this upcoming week?

_____

_____

What is ONE step that you will take this week to get closer to your dream?

_____

_____

Is there someone that could use your help this week? How can you make a
difference?

_____

Weekly Challenge 1

Take some time to clean out your purse and/or wallet.

Get things organized, file your receipts and put a little cash in there so that when you open it up you see money and feel
abundant.

Our minds (as brilliant as they are) cannot tell the difference between what is real and what we imagine—why not be a
millionaire?

Weekly Challenge 2

The challenge for this week is to go through all your bank accounts, mortgages and/or investments and make sure
everything is accurate (the bank accounts should be done monthly) and make sure that you have the right account for
your usage (you may need the help of your favourite banker).

Successful people know how and where their money is spent; do you?

Goals for this week

Health and Fitness

Love and Relationship

Career and Finance

Philanthropy and Giving Back

Shopping list

Hint:
Take a look at your one-year and three-month goals. How can you get closer to achieving them?

Doers and Shakers of the world

I've added a list of some of the incredible people that I have learned from and looked up to throughout my life. Some are inspirational speakers and motivators, most are philanthropist, some are financial advisors, some are actors, actresses and authors but ALL of them are people who have figured out the power they have within themselves and are changing the world in positive ways because of it. I encourage you to check them out!

Abraham. Ester & Jerry Hicks
Bob Proctor
Brendon Burchard
Brené Brown
Brian Tracy
Dean Graziosi
Donna Eden
Eckhart Tolle
Jim Carey
Joe Rogan
John Assaraf
Justin Perry
Karena & Katrina – Tone It Up
Lisa Nichols
Mel Robbins
Napoleon Hill
Oprah Winfrey
Richard Branson
Rhonda Byrnes
Robin Sharma
Tony Robbins
Vishen Lakhiani
Will Smith